A SELECT
BIBLIOGRAPHY
OF
GÜNTER GRASS
(From 1956 to 1973)

Photograph by Nancy Crampton

A Select

BIBLIOGRAPHY
OF
GÜNTER GRASS

(From 1956 to 1973)

INCLUDING

The Works, Editions, Translations, and Critical Literature.

By

Dr. George A. Everett, Jr.
Assistant Professor of Modern Languages
The University of Mississippi

BURT FRANKLIN, *Publishers*

Library of Congress Cataloging in Publication Data

Everett, George A. 1942-
    A bibliography of the works of Günter Grass.

    1. Grass, Günter, 1927- —Bibliography. I. Title.
Z8366.48.E93   016.838'9'1409   74-1420
ISBN 0-8337-5484-X

TABLE OF CONTENTS

LIST OF ILLUSTRATIONS

ABBREVIATIONS

Following those entries where it was deemed necessary, the following parenthetic abbreviations have been used to indicate subject matter:

(Au)	*Ausgefragt*
(TS)	*Aus dem Tagebuch einer Schnecke*
(Bt)	*Die Blechtrommel*
(BK)	*Die Bösen Köche*
(BG)	*Briefe über die Grenze*
(D)	*Davor*
(Gl)	*Gleisdreieck*
(Hw)	*Hochwasser*
(Hj)	*Hundejahre*
(KuM)	*Katz und Maus*
(NzM)	*Noch zehn Minuten bis Buffalo*
(öb)	*örtlich betäubt*
(öD)	*Eine öffentliche Diskussion*
(OO)	*Onkel, Onkel*
(Pl)	*Die Plebejer proben den Aufstand*
(ÜdS)	*Über das Selbstverständliche*
(Vo)	*Vogelscheuche*
(SH)	*Vom mangelnden Selbstvertrauen der schreibenden Hofnarren unter Berücksichtigung nicht vorhandener Höfe*
(VW)	*Die Vorzüge der Windhühner*
(Rev)	Book Review

PREFACE

The German author Günter Grass was born in Danzig, Poland, in 1927. He was, in turn, a member of the Hitler Youth, an artilleryman, and an eighteen-year-old prisoner of war. After the war he returned to civilian life, uneducated and without a job. He worked for a time as farm laborer, potash miner, stonemason apprentice, jazz musician and at other types of employment before enrolling as a student in the Art Academy at Düsseldorf and Berlin where he studied sculpture, painting and the graphic arts. His literary career dates from 1956 when he published his first book of poetry and had already begun to participate in the activities of the "Gruppe 47", a postwar avant-garde movement — as much political as literary — of authors and critics intent upon reviving German letters and ridding it of all vestiges of Nazi ideology. It was this group that awarded Grass its 1958 prize for his novel *Die Blechtrommel (The Tin Drum)*. Since then he has worked as a free-lance writer in France, Switzerland and West Germany, residing at present in West Berlin with his wife and four children.

Grass's social, religious, and political views are closely intertwined. In the light of his past experiences, he sees that the solution of man's troubles lies in self-reliance, buttressed by reason and a deep knowledge of history and its causes. It was this belief which led him into the political arena, on the side of Willy Brandt and the Social Democratic Party (SPD). He has been the most actively political writer in Germany since Walter von der Vogelweide, being attacked by both extremes of the Left and Right political parties for his middle-of-the-road position on contemporary issues. "As post-war Germany's most important, most outspoken novelist-poet-playwright, Grass has been clawing at the troubled conscience of his countrymen. Through biting sarcasm, trenchant allegories and wild Rabelaisian humor he has shattered the glittering facade of affluent West Germany to expose the deep-rooted guilt feelings and fears of the German people."[1]

Grass has used a wide variety of media as a forum for his views: poetry, novels, short stories, dramas, essays, political brochures, sculpture, drawings, the newspaper, radio, and television. From anonymity in 1955 to world fame in 1959 (with the publication of *Die Blechtrommel*), he has continued to be an author of great influence not only in Germany but also in most of the major literary centers of the world. Quite rightly he has been called "the most electrifying and revolutionary German writer of the age."[2] There is, in fact, every indication that Günter Grass will remain, along with Heinrich Böll, one of the pinnacles of German literature in the twentieth century.

The present bibliography — the fullest attempt to date — is intended to document the nature, extent and impact of Grass's literary publications as well as to trace the growing scholarly and popular interest in his thought and artistry. As such, it should prove useful not only to literary historians — especially those in the increasingly popular field of comparative and world literature — but to historians of contemporary social and political thought as well. Further, it is hoped that the separate listings of translations, besides showing the range of Grass's popularity, will be an aid to reference librarians serving those readers of their respective countries who are unfamiliar with German.

[1] Robinson, Donald. *The 100 most important people in the world today.* (New York, Putnam, 1970), p. 297.

[2] Willson, A. Leslie, editor. *A Günter Grass Symposium.* (Austin, Texas, 1971), pref.

WORKS
OF
GÜNTER GRASS

WORKS OF GÜNTER GRASS

1. Grass, Günter, "Abschusslisten," *Süddeutsche Zeitung,* München and *Der Abend*, Berlin (April 30 and May 1/2, 1971).

2. —————. "Adornos Zunge." *Akzente*, No. 4 (1965), p. 289.

3. —————. "An einen jungen Wähler, der sich versucht fühlt, NPD zu wählen," *Berliner Stimme* (November 26, 1966).

4. —————. "Die angelesene Revolution," foreword to Jens Litten, *Eine verpasste Revolution? Nachruf auf den SDS.* Hamburg, 1969.

5. —————. "Die angelesene Revolution," *frontal,* Bonn, No. 46 (Fall, 1968).

6. —————. "Der Arbeiter und seine Umwelt," Speech before the Deutschen Gewerkschaftsbund, Hamburg (May 1, 1971).

7. —————. "Auschwitz und Treblinka in Afrika," *Aufwärts*, Köln, No. 10 (1968).

8. —————. *Aus dem Tagebuch einer Schnecke.* Neuwied: Luchterhand, 1972.

9. —————. *Ausgefragt.* Neuwied: Luchterhand, 1967.

10. —————. *Die Ballerina.* Berlin: Friedenauer Presse, 1963.

11. —————. "Beim Kappenzählen," *Süddeutsche Zeitung,* München and *Der Abend,* Berlin (May 29/30/31, 1971).

12. —————. "Bequem auf dem Ast," *top*, Düsseldorf, No. 12 (1970).

13. —————. "Beritten Hin und Zurück," *Akzente*, No. 5 (1958), pp. 399ff.

14. —————. "Betroffen sein," *Der Abend*, Berlin (December 14, 1970).

15. —————. "Der Biedersinn gibt wieder den Ton an," *Blickpunkt*, Berlin (March, 1968).

16. —————. *Die Blechtrommel:* Neuwied: Luchterhand, March 1959

17. —————. "Blindlings," *Süddeutsche Zeitung*, München (October 31, 1970).

18. —————. *Die Bösen Köche*. Berlin: Kiepenheuer, 1961.

19. —————. "Die Bösen Köche," *Modernes deutsches Theater*. Vol. I. Ed. Paul Pörtner. Neuwied: Luchterhand, 1961, pp. 5-72.

20. —————. "Briefwechsel mit Klaus Schütz," *Telegraf*, Berlin (March 9, 1968).

21. —————. "Damals im Mai," *Süddeutsche Zeitung*, München (February 13, 1971).

22. —————. "Danach," Luchterhands Loseblatt Lyrik, No. 14 (1968).

23. —————. "Dank studentischer Lethargie," *Kölner Stadtanzeiger* (March 4, 1969). *Kölner Stadtanzeiger* (March 4, 1969).

24. —————. *Davor*. Berlin: Kiepenheuer, 1969.

25. —————. "Diese neue Regierung," *Die Zeit*, No. 50 (December 9, 1966).

26. —————. Drawings in, Ingeborg Bachmann. *Ein Ort für Zufälle*. Berlin: Wagenbach, 1965.

27. —————. "Die eigenen vier Wände," *Süddeutsche Zeitung*, München (October 17, 1970).

28. —————. "Eine Mahnung," *Der Abend*, Berlin (February 8, 1968).

29. —————. *Eine öffentliche Diskussion*. Hörspiel. Hessischer Rundfunk, 1963.

30. —————. "Eine Stimme won aussen her," *Vorwärts*, Bonn (March 28, 1968).

31. —————. "Eingemauert," *Westdeutsches Tageblatt* (February 24, 1962).

32. —————. "Ein glücklicher Mensch," *Süddeutsche Zeitung*, München (May 15/16, 1971).

33. —————. "Ein Sieg der Demokratie," *Die Neue Gesellschaft* (March/April, 1969).

34. —————. "Erklärung," *Münchner Merkur* (September 30, 1967).

35. —————. "Erklärung in der Sendung *Panorama*," *Norddeutscher Rundfunk* (September 25, 1967).

36. —————. "Die Erstgeburt," *Akzente*, No. 5 (1960), p. 435.

37. —————. *Es steht zur Wahl*. Neuwied: Luchterhand, 1965.

38. —————. Foreword to *Deutsche Parlamentsdebatten*. Vol. III. Ed. Eberhard Jäckel. Frankfurt am Main, 1971.

39. —————. "Fotogen," *Akzente*, No. 5 (1961), p. 450.

40. —————. "Freundliche Bitte um bessere Feinde," *Sprache im technischen Zeitalter* (1966), pp. 318ff.

41. —————. "Friedenspolitik in Spannungsfeldern," *Die Zeit*, No. 48 (November 22, 1968).

42. —————. *Fünf Köche*. Ballet, Choreography, M. Luipart. Aix-les-Bains and Bonn, 1959.

43. ——————. "Das Gelegenheitsgedicht oder—es ist immer noch, frei nach Picasso, verboten, mit dem Piloten zu sprechen," *Akzente* (1961), pp. 8ff.

44. ——————. "Genau hinsehen. Zum Tod des Bildhauers Karl Hartung," *Die Zeit*, No. 32 (August 4, 1967).

45. ——————. *Gesammelte Gedichte*. Intro. Heinrich Vormweg. Neuwied: Luchterhand, 1971.

46. ——————. "Gesamtdeutscher März," *Plädoyer für eine neue Regierung oder keine Alternative*. Ed. Hans Werner Richter. Reinbek: Rowohlt, 1965.   '

47. ——————. "Gewalttätigkeit ist wieder gesellschaftsfähig," *Der Spiegel*, XX, 20 (May 6, 1968).

48. ——————. "Das Gewissen der SPD," *Die Zeit*, No. 50 (December 9, 1966).

49. ——————. *Gleisdreieck*. Neuwied: Luchterhand, 1960.

50. ——————. "Goldmäulchen," Drama first produced in München, 1964, Werkraum Theater.

51. ——————. "Die Grosse Koalition ist zum Handeln aufgerufen," *Frankfurter Rundschau* (June 20, 1968).

52. ——————. *Günter Grass—Dich singe ich Demokratie"—Es Steht zur Wahl*. Phonograph Record, Köln-Braunsfeld: Carl Lindström Gesellschaft mbH, No. 12PAL2926ST.

53. ——————. *Günter Grass liest aus seinem Roman "Die Blechtrommel"*. Phonograph Record. Hamburg: Deutsche Grammophon Gesellschaft, No. 42012.

54. _____. *Günter Grass liest aus seinem Roman "örtlich betäubt" und Lyrik.* Phonograph Record. Hamburg: Deutsche Grammophon, No. 2575002.

55. _____. "Günter Grass und die Gewerkschaften. Eine kritische Mairede," *Welt der Arbeit*, Köln (May 16, 1969).

56. _____. "Harras macht Geschichte," *Das Atelier.* Frankfurt am Main: Fischer Bücherei, 1962, pp. 41-54.

57. _____. "Hochwasser: Erste Fassung," *Akzente,* No. 2 (1960), pp. 498ff.

58. _____. *Hochwasser.* Frankfurt am Main: Suhrkamp Verlag, 1963.

59. _____. *Hundejahre.* Neuwied: Luchterhand, 1963.

60. _____. "Ich bin dabeigewesen," *Frankfurter Rundschau* (May 10, 1968).

61. _____. "Ich bin gegen Radikalkuren," *Twen* (December, 1968).

62. _____. *Ich klage an!* Neuwied: Luchterhand, 1965.

63. _____. "Im Tunnel," *Nationalzeitung*, Basel (January 9, 1960).

64. _____. "In der Mauser," *Süddeutsche Zeitung*, München (February 27/28, 1971).

65. _____. "In Ermangelung," *Süddeutsche Zeitung*, München (January 16, 1971).

66. _____. "Der Inhalt als Widerstand," *Akzente*, No. 3 (1957), pp. 229-235.

67. _____. "In memoriam Walter Henn. Mein Freund Walter Henn ist tot," *Der Grüne Wagen*, München/Erlangen, 1963/1964.

68. —————. "In Kreuzberg fehlt ein Minarett," *Süddeutsche Zeitung*, München (January 30, 1971).

69. —————. "Jochen Steffen—meerumschlungen," *Der Abend*, Berlin (April 5, 1971).

70. —————. *Des Kaisers neue Kleider*. Neuwied: Luchterhand, 1965.

71. —————. *Katz und Maus*. Neuwied: Luchterhand, 1961.

72. —————. "Die Kinder der Melancolia," *Die Zeit*, No. 23 (June 13, 1972), p. 10.

73. —————. "Kleine Rede für Arno Schmidt," *Frankfurter Allgemeine Zeitung* (March 19, 1964).

74. —————. "Die kommunizierende Mehrzahl. Sollen die Deutschen eine Nation bilden?" *Süddeutsche Zeitung*, München (May 29, 1967).

75. —————. "Konflikte," *Frankfurter Rundschau* (February 3, 1969) and *Süddeutsche Zeitung*, München (February 3, 1969).

76. —————. "Kürzestgeschichten aus Berlin," *Akzente*, No. 6 (1955), pp. 517ff.

77. —————. "Der Lehrer an sich," *Man sage nicht, Lehrer hätten kein Herz*. Ed. Hans Eckart Rübesamen. München: Kindler Verlag GmbH, 1970, p. 331.

78. —————. "Lieber armer Freund Schlieker," *Sprache im technischen Zeitalter* (September, 1965).

79. —————. "Lilien aus Schlaf," *Akzente*, No. 3 (1955), pp. 259ff.

80. —————. "Die Linkshänder," *Neue Deutsche Hefte*, V, 1 (1958/1959), 38-42.

81. _____. "Die Linkshänder," *Deutschland Erzählt*. Frankfurt am Main: Fischer Bücherei, 1962, pp. 280-284.

82. _____. "Literatur und Revolution oder des Idyllikers schnaubendes Steckenpferd," Speech before the Schriftstellerkongress in Belgrad (October 17-21, 1969).

83. _____. *Loblied auf Willy*. Neuwied: Luchterhand, 1965.

84. _____. "Die Lüge," *Akzente*, No. 1 (1961).

85. _____. "Lyrik heute," *Akzente* (1961), pp. 2ff.

86. _____. "Der Mann mit der Fahne spricht einen atemlosen Bericht," *Akzente* (1965), pp. 122ff.

87. _____. "Meine grüne Wiese," *Akzente* (1955), pp. 528ff.

88. _____. "Mein Radiergummi," *Merkur*, No. 149 (1960).

89. _____. "Die melancholische Koalition," *Der Monat* (January, 1967).

90. _____. "Mit vierzig Mark begannen wir ein neues Leben," *Der Spiegel*, XX, 25 (June 10, 1968), 60ff.

91. _____. "Nachruf auf einen Gegner," *Stern* (May 8, 1967).

92. _____. "Nicht nur in eigener Sache," *Münchner Merkur* (October 24, 1968).

93. _____. *Noch zehn Minuten bis Buffalo*. Berlin: Kiepenheuer, 1957.

94. _____. *örtlich betäubt*. Neuwied: Luchterhand, 1969.

95. _____. "Offener Brief an Antonin Novotny," *Die Zeit*, No. 36 (September 5, 1967).

[Item no. 169]

Grass

Cat and Mouse

96. —————. "Offener Brief an Kurt Georg Kiesinger," *Frankfurter Allgemeine Zeitung* (December 1, 1966).

97. —————. "Offener Brief an Ludwig Erhard," *Spandauer Volksblatt*, Berlin (February 14, 1965).

98. —————. "Offener Brief an Siegfried Lenz," *Die Zeit*, No. 8 (February 16, 1962).

99. —————. "Ohrenbeichte: Brief an ein unbeschriebenes Blatt," *Sprache im technischen Zeitalter*, 2 (February, 1962), pp. 170ff.

100. —————. *Onkel, Onkel*. Berlin: Klaus Wagenbach Verlag, 1965.

101. —————. *O Susanna: Ein Jazz-Bilderbuch*. Köln: Kiepenheuer & Witsch, 1959.

102. —————. "Der Papiertiger," *Man sage nicht, Lehrer hätten kein Herz*. Ed. Hans Eckart Rübesamen. München: Kindler Verlag GmbH, 1970, p. 327.

103. —————. *Die Plebejer proben den Aufstand*. Neuwied: Luchterhand, 1966.

104. —————. "Poum oder die Vergangenheit fliegt mit," *Der Monat* (June, 1965), p. 21.

105. —————. "Rede an die Sozialdemokratische Bundestagsfraktion—23. März 1971," *Sozialdemokratische Wählerinitiative*. Bonn: Vorwärts-Druck, 1971.

106. —————. *Rede über das Selbstverständliche*. Neuwied: Luchterhand, 1965.

107. —————. "Rede von den begrenzten Möglichkeiten," *Club Voltaire IV*. Ed. Gerhard Szczesny. Reinbek bei Hamburg: Rowohlt Taschenbuch Verlag, 1970, pp. 145-156.

108. —————. "Rede von der Gewöhnung," *Frankfurter Allgemeine Zeitung,* Literaturblatt (March 20, 1967).

109. —————. "Die runde Zahl zwanzig," Speech given in Cloppenburg, September 28, 1969.

110. —————. "Schriftsteller und Gewerkschaft," *Einigkeit der Einzelgänger. Dokumentation des ersten Schriftstellerkongresses des Verbandes deutscher Schriftsteller.* Ed. Dieter Lattmann. München, 1971.

111. —————. "Schwierigkeiten eines Vaters, seinen Kindern Auschwitz zu erklären," *Der Tagesspiegel,* Berlin (May 27, 1970).

112. —————. "Der SDS verkennt die deutsche Lage," *Stuttgarter Nachrichten* (May 10, 1969).

113. —————. "Sollte dieser Preis zurückgewiesen werden?" *Die Zeit,* No. 7 (February 16, 1962), p. 6.

114. —————. "Stier oder Liebe," *Deutsche Zeitung,* Köln (October 9, 1960).

115. —————. *Stoffreste.* Ballet. Choreography, M. Luipart. Stadttheater Essen, 1957.

116. —————. "Teure Umwelt," *Süddeutsche Zeitung,* München (April 19, 1971).

117. —————. *Theaterspiele.* Neuwied: Luchterhand, 1970. (For plays contained, see entries #18, 24, 58, 93, 100, 103)

118. —————. "Toleranz ist unsere Stärke," *Die Zeit,* No. 6 (February 11, 1969), p. 3.

119. —————. "Tränentüchlein," *Der Telegraf,* Berlin (January 14, 1968).

120. —————. "Über das scheintote Theater," *Süddeutsche Zeitung,* München (June 13/14, 1970).

121. —————. "Über das Schreiben von Gedichten," *Lyrik unserer Zeit.* Ed. Horst Wolff. Dortmund, 1958.

122. —————. *Über das Selbstverständliche.* Neuwied: Luchterhand, 1968. (A collection of political speeches and politically motivated letters)

123. —————. "Über die erste Bürgerpflicht," *Die Zeit,* No. 3 (January 13, 1967).

124. —————. "Über Ja und Nein," *Die Zeit,* No. 51 (December 24, 1968), p. 9.

125. —————. "Über meinen Lehrer Döblin," *Akzente,* No. 14 (1968), pp. 290-309.

126. —————. *Über meinen Lehrer Döblin und andere Vorträge.* Berlin: Literarisches Colloquium Berlin, 1968. (For works contained, see entries #43, 66, 73, 125, 133, 135)

127. —————. "Uhuru heisst Freiheit . . . ,"*Süddeutsche Zeitung,* München (March 20/21, 1971).

128. —————. "Und was können die Schriftsteller tun?" *Die Zeit,* No. 34 (August 18, 1961).

129. —————. "Unser Grundübel ist der Idealismus," *Der Spiegel,* XXIII, 33 (August 11, 1969), 94.

130. —————. "Verlorene Provinzen—gewonnene Einsicht," *Süddeutsche Zeitung,* München and *Der Abend,* Berlin (November 30, 1970).

131. —————. "Völkermord vor aller Augen. Ein Appell an die Bundesregierung," *Die Zeit,* No. 41 (October 3, 1968), p. 5.

132. —————. *Die Vogelscheuchen.* Ballet. Choreography, M. Luipart. Deutsche Oper Berlin, 1970.

133. _____. "Vom mangelnden Selbstvertrauen der schreibenden Hofnarren unter Berücksichtigung nicht vorhandener Höfe," *Akzente*, No. 13 (1966) pp. 194-199.

134. _____. "Von draussen nach drinnen," *Der Spiegel*, XX, 47 (November 14, 1966), 56.

135. _____. "Vor-und Nachgeschichte der Tragödie des Coriolanus von Livius und Plutarch über Shakespeare bis zu Brecht und mir," *Akzente*, No. 11 (1964), pp. 194-221.

136. _____. *Die Vorzüge der Windhühner*. Berlin: Luchterhand, 1956.

137. _____. "Warnung vor Demagogen von rechts und links," *Neue Ruhr-Zeitung*, Essen (May 18, 1969).

138. _____. "Was Erfurt ausserdem bedeutet," Speech in Baden-Baden (May 1, 1970).

139. _____. *Was ist des deutschen Vaterland*. Neuwied: Luchterhand, 1965.

140. _____. "Was lesen die Soldaten?" *Weser-Kurier*, Bremen (May 17, 1969).

141. _____. "Was nicht vom Himmel fällt," *Süddeutsche Zeitung*, München and *Der Abend*, Berlin (January 2, 1971).

142. _____. "Was unterm Strich steht," *Stuttgarter Zeitung* (December 31, 1968).

143. _____. "Wer wird dieses Bändchen kaufen?" *Die Alternative oder Brauchen wir eine neue Regierung*. Ed. Martin Walser. Reinbek: Rowohlt, 1961.

144. _____. "Wie frei wird in Bayern gewählt?" *Süddeutsche Zeitung*, München (November 14/15, 1970).

145. ⸻. "Willy Brandt und die Friedensenzyklika," *Süddeutsche Zeitung*, München (November 11, 1966).

146. ⸻. "Wir haben nicht die demokratische Reife," *Frankfurter Rundschau* (April 14, 1968).

147. ⸻. "Zum Zwischenfall in der "Schaubühne'," *Die Welt* (June 4, 1971).

148. ⸻. *Zweiunddreissig Zähne*. Berlin: Kiepenheuer, 1958.

149. ⸻. "Zwischen den Terminen," *Süddeutsche Zeitung*, München (October 3, 1970).

150. Grass, Günter, *et al. Der Fall Axel C. Springer am Beispiel Arnold Zweig*. Voltaire Flugschrift No. 15. Ed. Bernward Vesper. Berlin: Voltaire Verlag, 1967.

151. Grass, Günter and Pavel Kohout. *Briefe über die Grenze: Versuch eines Ost-West Dialoges*. Die Zeit Bücher. Hamburg: Christian Wegner Verlag GmbH, 1968.

152. Grass, Günter and Uwe Johnson. "Conversation with Simonov," *Encounter*, XXIV, 1 (January, 1965), 88-91.

153. Grass, Günter and Willy Brandt. "Offener Briefwechsel mit Willy Brandt," *Die Zeit*, Nos. 49 and 50 (December 2, 1966 and December 9, 1966).

154. Grass, Günter and Wolfdietrich Schnurre. "Offener Brief an den Deutschen Schriftstellerverband," *Die Zeit*, No. 33 (August 18, 1961), p. 14.

TRANSLATIONS
BY
LANGUAGE

CZECHOSLOVAKIAN

155. Grass, Günter. *Kocka a Mys.* Trans. Zlujnek Sekal. Prague: Odeon, 1968. (KuM)

156. ⸻. *Plechový Bubínek.* Trans. Vladimir Kafka. Prague: Mladá fronta, 1969. (Bt)

157. ⸻. "Povoden," *Západonemecké Moderní Drama.* Trans. Jitka Bodláková and Jirí Stach. Prague: Orbis, 1969, pp. 6-53. (Hw)

158. ⸻. *Zlí Kuchari.* Trans. Jan Tomek. Prague: Dilia, 1967. (BK)

CZECHOSLOVAKIAN (SLOVENIAN)

159. ⸻. *Macka a Mys.* Trans. Perla Bzochová. Bratislava: Slov. spis, 1966. (KuM)

DANISH

160. ⸻. *Bliktrommen.* Trans. Mogens Boisen. Copenhagen: Gyldendal, 1961. (Bt)

161. ⸻. *Hundear.* Trans. Mogens Boisen. Copenhagen: Gyldendal, 1965. (Hj)

162. ⸻. *Kat og Mus* Trans. Mogens Boisen. Copenhagen: Gyldendal, 1963. (KuM)

DUTCH

163. ⸻. *De Blikken Trommel.* Trans. Koos Schuur. Amsterdam: J. M. Meulenhoff, 1964. (Bt)

164. —————. *Hondejaren*. Trans. Koos Schuur. Amsterdam: J. M. Meulenhoff, 1965. (Hj)

165. —————. *Kat en Muis*. Trans. Hermien Manger. Amsterdam: J. M. Meulenhoff, 1963. (KuM)

166. —————. *Plaatselijk Verdoofd*. Trans. C. Schuur-Kaspers. Amsterdam: J. M. Meulenhoff, 1969. (öb)

ENGLISH

167. —————. *Cat and Mouse*. Trans. Ralph Manheim. London: Secker & Warburg, 1963. (KuM)

168. —————. *Cat and Mouse*. Trans. Ralph Manheim. Toronto: New American Library of Canada, 1964. (KuM)

169. —————. *Cat and Mouse*. Trans. Ralph Manheim. New York: Harcourt, Brace, and World, 1963. (KuM)

170. —————. "Crack-up," "In the Egg," "Frost and Bite," "The Ballad of the Black Cloud," "To all the Gardeners" trans. J. Rothenberg. *Evergreen Review*, XXXII (April/May, 1964), 67-69.

171. —————. *Dog Years*. Trans. Ralph Manheim. London: Seeker & Warburg, 1965. (Hj)

172. —————. *Dog Years*. Trans. Ralph Manheim. New York: Harcourt, Brace, and World, 1965. (Hj)

173. —————. "Draussen," *Atlas,* XIII, 3 (March, 1967), 65-66.

174. —————. *Four Plays*. Trans. Ralph Manheim and A. Leslie Willson. Ed. and intro. Martin Esslin. New York: Harcourt, Brace, and World, 1967. (Hw, OO, NzM, BK)

175. _____. *Four Plays*. Trans. Ralph Manheim and A. Leslie Willson. London: Secker & Warburg, 1968. (Hw, OO, NzM, BK)

176. _____. *From the Diary of a Snail*. Trans. Ralph Manheim. New York: Harcourt Brace Jovanovich, Inc., 1973. (TS)

177. _____. "Grass Speaks," *Atlas*, XI, 4 (April, 1966), 250.

178. _____. "In the Egg," *Nation*, CCI (August 16, 1965), 82.

179. _____. *Local Anaesthetic*. Trans. Ralph Manheim. New York: Harcourt, Brace, and World, 1970. (öb)

180. _____. *Local Anaesthetic*. Trans. Ralph Manheim. London: Secker & Warburg, 1970. (öb)

181. _____. *Max*. Trans. A. Leslie Willson and Ralph Manheim. New York: Harcourt Brace Jovanovich, Inc., 1972. (D)

182. _____. "Midge Plague," Trans. Christopher Middleton. *London Times Literary Supplement*, 3213 (September 27, 1963), p. 732.

183. _____. *New Poems*. Trans. Michael Hamburger. New York: Harcourt, Brace, and World, 1968. (Au)

184. _____. "Open Wardrobe," Trans. Michael Hamburger, *Poetry*, XCVIII (June, 1961), 154.

185. _____. "On the Lack of Self-confidence of the Literary Court Jester without a Court," *American German Review*, XXXII, 5 (1965/1966), 20-22. (SH)

186. _____. "Open Letter to Kurt Kiesinger," *Nation*, CCIV, 7 (February 13, 1967), 214.

187. _____. *The Plebeians Rehearse the Uprising.* Trans. Ralph Manheim. New York: Harcourt, Brace, and World, 1966. (Pl)

188. _____. *The Plebeians Rehearse the Uprising.* Trans. Ralph Manheim. London: Secker & Warburg, 1968. (Pl)

189. _____. "The Salt Lake Line," Trans. and adapted by Christopher Holme. *German Writing Today.* Ed. Christopher Middleton. Middlesex: Penguin Books, Ltd., 1967, pp. 61-78. (NzM)

190. _____. *Selected Poems.* Trans. Michael Hamburger and Christopher Middleton. London: Secker & Warburg, 1966. (VW and Gl)

191. _____. *Selected Poems.* Trans. Michael Hamburger and Christopher Middleton. New York: Harcourt, Brace, and World, 1967. (VW and Gl)

192. _____. *Speak Out!* Trans. Ralph Manheim. New York: Harcourt, Brace, and World, 1967. (ÜdS)

193. _____. *The Tin Drum.* Trans. Ralph Manheim. New York: Harcourt, Brace, and World, 1961. (Bt)

194. _____. *The Tin Drum.* Trans. Ralph Manheim. London: Secker & Warburg, 1961. (Bt)

195. _____. "Transformation," Trans. Michael Hamburger. *London Times Literary Supplement*, 3111 (October 13, 1961), p. 725.

196. _____. "Unsuccessful Raid," "Family Matters," Trans. Michael Hamburger. *Evergreen Review*, XXXVI (June, 1965), 93.

197. ⸻. *Uptight*, Scenes 1, 3, 5, 6. Trans. A. Leslie Willson. *Dimension*, III, Special Issue (1970), 91-123. (D)

198. ⸻. "The Wide Skirt," Trans. Ralph Manheim, *Evergreen Review*, V, 21 November/December, 1961), 36-44.

FINNISH

199. ⸻. *Kissa ja Hiiri*. Trans. Aarno Peromies. Helsinki: Otava, 1962. (KuM)

200. ⸻. *Koiranvuosia*. Trans. Aarno Peromies. Helsinki: Otava, 1964. (Hj)

201. ⸻. Peltirumpu. Trans. Aarno Peromies. Helsinki: Otava, 1961. (Bt)

FRENCH

202. ⸻. *Les Années de Chien*. Trans. Jean Amsler. Paris: Éditions du Seuil, 1965. (Hj)

203. ⸻. *Le Chat et la Souris*. Trans. Jean Amsler. Paris: Éditions du Seuil, 1962. (KuM)

204. ⸻. *Le Chat et la Souris*. Trans. Jean Amsler. Lausanne: La Guilde du livre, 1966. (KuM)

205. ⸻. *Évidences politiques*. Trans. Jean Amsler, Luc de Goustine, and Bernard Lortholary. Paris: Éditions du Seuil, 1969. (ÜdS)

206. ⸻. *Les Plébéiens répètent l'insurrection*. Trans. Jean Amsler. Paris: Éditions du Seuil, 1968. (Pl)

207. ⸻. *Le Tambour*. Trans. Jean Amsler. Paris: Éditions du Seuil, 1961. (Bt)

208. Grass, Günter and Pavel Kohout. *Lettres pardessus la Frontière*. Trans. Richard Dentruck. Paris: C. Bourgois, 1969. (BG)

HUNGARIAN

209. Grass, Günter. *Macska ës Egér*. Trans. Elga Sárközy. Budapest: Európa Kiadó, 1968 (KuM)

210. —————. *Vallató*. Trans. Balázs Boldog, *et al*. Budapest: Európa Kiadó, 1969. (ÜdS)

ITALIAN

211. —————. *Anni di Cani*. Trans. Enrico Filippini. Milan: Feltrinelli, 1966. (Hj)

212. —————. *Gatto e Topo*. Trans. Enrico Filippini. Milan: Feltrinelli, 1967. (KuM)

213. —————. *Il Tamburo di Latta*. Trans. Lia Secci. Milan: Feltrinelli, 1965. (Bt)

214. —————. *Tutto il Teatro (I plebei provano la rivolta, Acqua alta, A dieci minuti da Buffalo, Una discussione pubblica)*. Trans. Enrico Filippini. Milan: Feltrinelli, 1968. (Pl, Hw, NzM, ÖD)

JAPANESE

215. —————. *Buriki no Taiko*. Trans. Takamoto Ken'ichi. Tokyo: Shûeisha, 1967. (Bt)

216. —————. *Inu no Toshi*. Trans. Nakano Kôji. Tokyo: Shûeisha, 1969. (Hj)

217. —————. *Jimei no Koto ni Tsuite*. Trans. Takomoto Ken'ichi and Miyahara Akira. Tokyo: Shûeisha, 1970 (ÜdS)

218. —————. *Neko to Nezumi*. Trans. Takamoto Ken'ichi. Tokyo: Shûeisha, 1968. (KuM)

NORWEGIAN

219. —————. *Blikktrommen*. Trans. Trygve Greiff. Oslo: Gyldendal, 1960. (Bt)

220. —————. *Hundeår*. Trans. Hans Braarvig. Oslo: Gyldendal, 1965. (Hj)

221. —————. *Katt og Mus*. Trans. Trygve Greiff. Oslo: Gyldendal, 1962. (KuM)

POLISH

222. —————. *Kot i Mysz*. Trans. Irena Naganowska and Egon Naganowski. Warsaw: Cytelnik, 1963. (KuM)

PORTUGUESE

223. —————. *O Cão de Hitler*. Trans. Lídia de Castro. Lisbon: Cor, 1966. (Hj)

224. —————. *O Gato e o Rato*. Trans. Carmen Gonzalez. Lisbon: Europa- América, 1968. (KuM)

225. —————. *O Tambor*. Trans. Augusto Abelaira. Lisbon: Cor, 1964. (Bt)

SPANISH

226. —————. *El Gato y el Ratón*. Trans. Carlos Gerhard. Mexico: Joaquín Mortiz, 1964. (KuM)

227. —————. *Los Plegeyos ensayan la Rebelión*. Trans. Heleno Saña Alcón. Madrid: Edicusa, 1969. (Pl)

228. —————. *El Tambor de Hojalata*. Trans. Carlos Gerhard. Mexico: Joaquin Mortiz, 1963. (Bt)

SPANISH (CATALONIAN)

229. —————. *El Gat i la Rata*. Trans. Carles Unterlohner. Barcelona: Ediciones 62, 1968. (KuM)

SWEDISH

230. —————. *Blektrumman.* Trans. Nils Holmberg. Stockholm: Bonnier, 1961. (Bt)

231. —————. *Hundår.* Trans. Lars W. Freij. Stockholm: Bonnier, 1965. (Hj)

232. —————. *Katt och Råtta.* Trans. John W. Walldén. Stockholm: Bonnier, 1962. (KuM)

233. —————. *Lokalbedövad.* Trans. Ingrid Rüegger and Eva Liljegren. Stockholm: Bonnier, 1970. (öb)

234. —————. *Plebejerna repeterar upproret.* Trans. Per E. Wahlund. Stockholm: Bonnier, 1967. (Pl)

TURKISH

235. —————. *On Dakka sonra Buffalo.* Trans. Adalet Cimcoz. Istanbul: Istanbul Matbassi, 1964. (NzM)

YUGOSLAVIAN

236. —————. *Decji Dobos* (I/II). Trans. Olga Trebicnik. Novi Sad: Bratstvo-jedinstvo, 1963, 2 vols. (Bt)

237. —————. *Macka i Mis.* Trans. Mira Buljan. Zagreb: Zora, 1969. (KuM)

238. —————. *Pseće Godine.* Trans. Ivan Ivanji. Belgrade: Prosveta, 1965, 2 vols. (Hj)

YUGOSLAVIAN (SLOVIAN)

239. —————. *Plocevinasti Boben.* Trans. Janko Moder. Ljubljana: Drzavna Zalozba Slovenije, 1968, 2 vols. (Bt)

CRITICAL LITERATURE

CRITICAL LITERATURE

BOOKS

240. Ahl, Herbert. "Ohne Scham, ohne Tendenz, ohne Devise: Günter Grass," *Literarische Porträts.* München: Langen/Müller, 1962, pp. 28-35.

241. Albrecht, Günter, Kurt Böttcher, *et al.* "Günter Grass," *Deutsches Schriftstellerlexikon von den Anfängen bis zur Gegenwart.* Weimar: Volksverlag Weimar, 1964, pp. 215-216.

242. Arnold, Heinz Ludwig and Franz Josef Görtz. *Günter Grass: Dokumente zur politischen Wirkung.* Stuttgart: Boorberg Verlag, 1971. (For articles contained, see entries #1, 5, 6, 11, 15, 25, 30, 34, 35, 46, 60, 64, 82, 92, 96, 105, 109, 112, 113, 128, 130, 138, 141, 142, 143, 146, 147, 153, 346, 348, 360, 362, 368, 373, 381, 384, 396, 397, 407, 409, 427, 431, 432, 434, 436, 441, 451, 454, 456, 473, 480, 483, 490, 496, 514, 517, 525, 527, 535, 537, 566, 569, 573, 575, 576, 580, 581, 597, 608, 614, 618, 628, 639, 645, 651, 657, 658, 665, 671, 675, 678, 684, 686, 693, 718, 720, 722, 740, 747, 748, 755, 757, 766, 768, 769, 773, 780, 821, 822, 838, 839, 841, 842, 850, 859, 860, 862, 863, 866, 867, 869, 870, 872, 880, 882, 894, 901, 902, 910, 912, 916, 920, 921, 927, 928, 945 950, 952, 953, 958, 962, 963, 966, 967, 973, 999, 1000, 1011)

243. Bettex, Albert. "Die moderne Literatur," *Deutsche Literaturgeschichte in Grundzügen.* Ed. Bruno Boesch. 3rd ed. München: Franke Verlag, 1967, p. 474.

244. Bieneck, Horst. *Günter Grass.* Reihe Werkstattgespräche mit Schriftstellern. München: Langen/Müller, 1962.

245. Blöcker, Günter. "Günter Grass: *Die Blechtrommel,*" *Kritisches Lesebuch.* Hamburg: Leibniz Verlag, 1962, pp. 208-215.

246. —————. "Günter Grass: *Hundejahre,*" *Literatur als Teilhabe.* Berlin: Colloquium Verlag, 1966, pp. 24-29.

247. Bobrowski, Johannes. "Die Windhühner," *Das Buch von drüben,* in the foreword by Johannes Bobrowski. Berlin: Altberliner Verlag, 1957.

248. Bräutigam, K. "Günter Grass: 'Freitag'," *Moderne deutsche Balladen.* Frankfurt am Main: M. Diederichs Verlag, 1971, pp. 62-101.

249. Brinkmann, Hennig. "Der komplexe Satz im deutschen Schrifttum der Gegenwart," *Sprachkunst als Weltgestaltung: Festschrift.* Ed. Herbert Seidler, 1966, pp. 12-26.

250. Büscher, Heiko. "Günter Grass," *Deutsche Literatur seit 1945.* Ed. Dietrich Weber. Stuttgart: Kröner Verlag, 1968, pp. 455-483.

251. Cunliffe, W. Gordon. *Günter Grass.* Twayne's World Authors Series. New York: Twayne Publishers, Inc., 1969.

252. Diederichs, Rainer. *Strukturen des Schelmischen im modernen deutschen Roman: eine Untersuchung an den Romanen von Thomas Mann "Bekenntnisse des Hochstaplers Felix Krull" und Günter Grass "Die Blechtrommel."* Düsseldorf: E. Diesterweg Verlag, 1968, pp. 94-99.

253. Durzak, Manfred. *Arno Holz, Alfred Döblin, Günter Grass. Zur Tradition von politischer Dichtung in Deutschland.* Saltsjö-Duvnås Sweden: Moderna språk, 1971.

GÜNTER GRASS

SPEAK OUT!

SPEECHES,

OPEN LETTERS,

COMMENTARIES

INTRODUCTION BY

MICHAEL HARRINGTON

[Item no. 192]

254. —————. "Fiktion und Gesellschaftsanalyse, Die Romane von Günter Grass," *Der deutsche Roman der Gegenwart.* Stuttgart: W. Kohlhammer Verlag, 1971, pp. 107-173.

255. Edschmid, Kasimir. "Gutachten," *Von Buch zu Buch.* Ed. Gert Loschütz. Neuwied: Luchterhand, 1968, pp. 60-61.

256. Emmel, Hildegard. "Das Selbstgericht: Thomas Mann, Walter Jens, und Eduard Schaper, Günter Grass," *Das Gericht in der deutschen Literatur des 20. Jahrhunderts.* München: Franke Verlag, 1963, pp. 82-119.

257. Engel, Erich. *Schriften über Theater und Film.* Berlin: Henschelverlag, 1971, pp. 112ff.

258. Enright, Dennis Joseph. "Dog Years," *Conspirators and Poets.* London: Chatto and Windus, 1966, pp. 201-207.

259. —————. "Three New Germans," *Conspirators and Poets.* London: Chatto and Windus, 1966, pp. 190-200.

260. Enzensberger, Hans Magnus. "Gutachten," *Von Buch zu Buch.* Ed. Gert Loschütz. Neuwied: Luchterhand, 1968, pp. 61-64.

261. —————. "Katz und Maus," *Einzelheiten.* Frankfurt: Suhrkamp Verlag, 1962, pp. 227-233.

262. —————. "Wilhelm Meister auf Blech getrommelt," *Einzelheiten.* Frankfurt: Suhrkamp Verlag, 1962, pp. 221-227.

263. Esslin, Martin, ed. "Günter Grass," *Sinn oder Unsinn? Das Groteske im modernen Drama.* Basel: Basilius Presse, 1962, pp. 40-44.

264. —————. "Günter Grass" *Le Theâtre de l' Absurde.* Paris: Buchet-Chastel, 1963, pp. 262-264.

265. Eykman, Christoph. *Geschichtspessimus in der deutschen Literatur des zwanzigsten Jahrhunderts.* Bern: Franke Verlag, 1970, pp. 64-68.

266. Fehse, Willi. *Von Goethe bis Grass: Biographische Porträts zur Literatur.* Bielefeld: Gieseking Verlag, 1963, pp. 227-231.

267. Forster, Leonard. "Kirschen," *Doppelinterpretationen.* Frankfurt: Athenäum, 1966, pp. 276-280.

268. Fricke-Klotz, W. "Günter Grass," *Geschichte der deutschen Dichtung.* Hamburg, 1966, pp. 492-494.

269. Gaus, Günter. "Manche Freundschaft zerbrach am Ruhm," *Zur Person: Porträts in Frage und Antwort, II.* München: Feder Verlag, 1966, pp. 110-122.

270. Goetze, Albrecht. "Die Hundertdritte und tiefunterste Materniade: Bemerkungen zum Roman *Hundejahre* von Günter Grass anhand des Schlusskapitels," *Vergleichen und Verändern. Festschrift für Helmut Motekat.* Ed. Albrecht Goetze and Günther Pflaum. München: Max Hueber, 1970, pp. 273-277.

271. _____. *Pression und Deformation.* Reihe Göppingener Arbeiten zur Germanistik, No. 74.Göppingen: A Kümmerle, 1972.

272. Grunert, Manfred and Barbara Grunert, eds. "Schulklassengespräch mit Günter Grass am 10.12.1963 in der Albert-Schweitzer-Oberschule in Berlin-Neukölln," *Wie stehen Sie Dazu? Jugend fragt Prominente.* München: Max Hueber Verlag, 1967, pp. 74-86.

273. "Günter Grass," *Eckart Jahrbuch.* Ed. Kurt Lothar Tank. Vol. IV, 1963/1964. Witten and Berlin: Eckart Verlag, 1963, pp. 299-304.

274. Hatfield, Henry. "The Artist as Satirist," *The Contemporary Novel in German: A Symposium.* Ed Robert R. Heitner. Austin, Texas: University of Texas Press, 1967, pp. 115-134.

275. —————. *Crisis and Continuity in Modern German Fiction: Ten Essays.* Ithaca, New York: Cornell University Press, 1968, pp. 128-149.

276. Holthusen, Hans Egon. "Günter Grass als politischer Autor," *Plädoyer für den Einzelnen.* München: Nymphenburger Verlagshandlung, 1967, pp. 40-68.

277. Horst, Karl August. *Anatomy and Trends of 20th Century German Literature.* Trans. Elizabeth Thompson. München: Nymphenburger Verlagshandlung, 1964, pp. 94 *et passim.*

278. —————. "Günter Grass," *Kleines Handbuch der deutschen Gegenwartsliteratur.* Ed. Hermann Kunisch. München: Nürnburger Verlagshandlung, 1967, pp. 181-187.

279. —————. *Kritischer Führer durch die deutsche Literatur der Gegenwart.* München: Nymphenburger Verlagshandlung, 1962, pp. 149ff.

280. Hyman, Stanley Edgar. "An Inept Symbolist: Günter Grass," *Standards: A Chronicle of Books for our Time.* New York: Horizon Press, 1966, pp. 168-172.

281. Ihlenfeld, Kurt. "Rarität und Realität," *Eckart Jahrbuch.* Vol. III, 1961. Witten and Berlin: Eckart Verlag, 1961, pp. 278-280.

282. Ivey, Frederick M. *The Tin Drum; or, Retreat to the Word.* University Studies No. 66. Wichita, Kansas: Wichita State University Press, 1966.

283. Jens, Walter. "Gutachten," *Von Buch zu Buch.* Ed. Gert Loschütz. Neuwied: Luchterhand, 1968, pp. 64-65.

284. Just, G. *Darstellungsaesthetik versus Wirkungsaesthetik*. München: Athenäum, 1972.

285. Kaiser, G. *Günter Grass "Katz und Maus"*. München: Fink, 1971.

286. Kaiser, J. "Günter Grass oder das erfüllte Image," *Führer und Verführer. Geist und Mode unserer Zeit*. Eds. L. Reinisch and K. Hoffman. München: Droemer-Knaur, 1971, pp. 193-205.

287. Kesting, Marianne. "Günter Grass," *Panorama des zeitgenössischen Theaters*. München: R. Piper Verlag, 1962, pp. 253-261.

288. Kienecker, Friedrich. "Günter Grass: 'Im Ei'," *Der Mensch in der modernen Lyrik*. Düsseldorf: A. Henn Verlag, 1970, pp. 97-105.

289. Knudsen, Jorgen. "Günter Grass," *Fremmede digtere idet 20. århundrede*. Vol. III. Ed. Sven M. Kristensen. Copenhagen: G. E. C. Grad, 1968, pp. 551-568.

290. Kunisch, Hermann, ed. *Handbuch der deutschen Gegenwartsliteratur*. München: Nürnberger Verlagshandlung, 1965, pp. 216-217.

291. *Kunst oder Pornographie? Der Prozess Grass gegen Ziesel. Eine Dokumentation*. 2nd ed. Müchen: Lehmann Verlag, 1969.

292. Kurz, Paul Konrad. "*Hundejahre*: Beobachtungen zu einem zeitkritischen Roman," *Über moderne Literatur*. Frankfurt am Main: Verlag Josef Knecht, 1967, pp. 158-176.

293. —————. "*Hundejahre*: Some Remarks about a Novel of Contemporary Criticism," *On Modern German Literature*. Vol. I. Trans. Sister Mary Frances McCarthy. University, Alabama: The University of Alabama Press, 1970. pp. 131-148.

294. _____. *Über moderne Literatur: Standorte und Deutungen.* Vol. I. Frankfurt am Main: Verlag Josef Knecht, 1967, pp. 158-176.

295. _____. "Windhühner ausgefragt. Zur Lyrik von Günter Grass," *Über moderne Literatur,* Vol. II. Frankfurt am Main: Verlag Josef Knecht, 1969, pp. 237-164.

296. Lennartz, Franz. "Günter Grass," *Deutsche Dichter und Schriftsteller unserer Zeit.* Stuttgart: Alfred Kröner Verlag, 1963, pp. 231-233.

297. Lettau, Reinhard, ed. *Die Gruppe 47: Ein Handbuch.* Neuwied: Luchterhand, 1967, pp. 136-138 *et passim.*

298. Loschütz, Gert, ed. *Von Buch zu Buch: Günter Grass in der Kritik.* Neuwied: Luchterhand, 1968. (For articles contained, see entries #247, 255, 260, 262, 283, 302, 372, 383, 390, 400, 402, 416, 417, 426, 438, 443, 446, 463, 468, 484, 503, 532, 543, 546, 560, 561, 563, 587, 591, 596, 603, 612, 617, 619, 626, 629, 630, 632, 634, 636, 644, 646, 650, 660, 680, 689, 692, 719, 727, 735, 736, 745, 749, 758, 785, 789, 792, 794, 801, 802, 824, 825, 836, 857, 877, 883, 891, 908, 909, 929, 940, 944, 948, 955, 956, 961, 980, 981, 990, 997, 1012, 1020, 1023, 1032, 1033, 1034, 1035, 1036)

299. Lukács G. *Die Theorie des Romans.* 2nd ed. Neuwied: Luchterhand, 1963, pp. 53 *et passim.*

300. Mandel, Siegfried. "The German Novel: In the Wake of Organized Madness," *Contemporary European Novelists.* Carbondale: Southern Illinois University Press, 1968, pp. 69-125.

301. Martini, Fritz. *Deutsche Literaturgeschichte von den Anfängen bis zur Gegenwart.* Stuttgart: Alfred Kröner Verlag, 1960, p. 603.

302. _____. "Gutachten," *Von Buch zu Buch.* Ed. Gert Loschütz. Neuwied: Luchterhand, 1968, pp. 58-60.

303. Mayer, Hans. "Felix Krull und Oskar Matzerath. Aspekte des Romans," *Das Geschehen und das Schweigen: Aspekte der Literatur.* Frankfurt am Main: Suhrkamp Verlag, 1969, pp. 35-76.

304. _____. *Zur deutschen Literatur der Zeit.* Reinbek: Rowohlt, 1967, pp. 56 *et passim.*

305. Moore, Harry T. *Twentieth Century German Literature.* London: Heinemann Educational Books, Ltd., 1971, pp. 200-206.

306. Müller, André. "Ein Anti-Grass Stück," *Nachrichtenbrief 35, Arbeitskreis Bertold Brecht.* Köln, 1966.

307. O'Nan, Martha. *Günter Grass' Oskar.* Occasional Papers in Language, Literature, and Linguistics, A3, Ohio University. Athens: Ohio University Modern Language Department, 1967.

308. _____. *The Role of Mind in Hugo, Faulkner, Beckett, and Grass.* New York: Philosophical Library, 1969, pp. 36-48.

309. Piirainen, Ilpo Tapani. *Textbezogene Untersuchungen über "Katz und Maus" und "Hundejahre" von Günter Grass.* Europäische Hochschulschriften: Reihe 1: Deutsche Literatur und Germanistic, XI. Bern: Lang Verlag, 1968.

310. Piontek, Heinz. "Günter Grass," *Männer, die Gedichte machen.* 1970, pp. 179-202.

311. Pongs, Hermann. "Günter Grass," *Dichtung im gespaltenen Deutschland.* Stuttgart: Union Verlag, 1966, pp. 36ff.

312. Pross, H. "Kritik als Fürsprache. Günter Grass," *Söhne der Kassandra,* 1971, pp. 131-141.

313. Reich-Ranicki, Marcel. "Günter Grass: *Ausgefragt*," *Literatur der kleinen Schritte*. München: R. Piper Verlag, 1971, pp. 203-208.

314. _____. "Günter Grass: *Hundejahre*," *Literatur der kleinen Schritte*. München: R. Piper Verlag, 1971, pp. 21-30.

315. _____. "Günter Grass: *Die Plebejer proben den Aufstand*," *Literatur der Kleinen Schritte*. München: R. Piper Verlag, 1971, pp. 130-134.

316. _____. "Günter Grass, unser grimmiger Idylliker," *Deutsche Literatur in West und Ost*. München: R. Piper Verlag, 1963, pp. 116-130.

317. Richter, Hans Werner, ed. *Die Mauer oder der 13. August*. Reinbek: Rowohlt Verlag, 1961.

318. Rudolph, Ekkehardt, ed. *Protokoll zur Person. Autoren über sich und ihr Werk*. München: List, 1971, pp. 59-72.

319. Salyámosy, Miklós. "Günter Grass," *A Német irodalom a XX. században*. Budapest: Gondolat, 1966, pp. 493-507.

320. Schwarz, Wilhelm Johannes. *Der Erzähler Günter Grass*. Bern: A. Franke Verlag, 1969.

321. Sodeikat, Ernst. *Schrieb Günter Grass eine Danzig-Saga? Ergebnisse einer Analyse der Bücher "Die Blechtrommel" und "Hundejahre"*. Hannover: Bergward Verlag, 1969.

322. Steiner, George. "A Note on Günter Grass," *Language and Silence*. New York: Atheneum, 1967, pp. 110-117.

323. Stutz, Elfriede. "Studien über Herr und Hund. Maria von Ebner-Eschenbach, Thomas Mann, Günter Grass," *Das Tier in der Dichtung*, 1970, pp. 200-238.

324. Subiotto, Arrigo. "Günter Grass," *Essays on Contemporary German Literature*. Ed. Brian Keith-Smith. German Men of Letters Series, Vol. IV. Philadelphia: Dufour, 1966, pp. 215-235.

325. Tank, Kurt Lothar. *Günter Grass*. Berlin: Colloquium Verlag, 1965.

326. —————. *Günter Grass*. New York: Ungar, 1969.

327. —————. *Günter Grass*. 4th rev. ed. Berlin: Colloquium Verlag, 1971.

328. Thomas, R. Hinton and Wilfried van der Will. "Günter Grass," *The German Novel and the Affluent Society*. Toronto: Victoria College Press, 1968, pp. 68-85.

329. Tiesler, Ingrid. *Günter Grass: "Katz und Maus"*. Reihe Interpretationen zum Deutschunterricht. Eds. Rupert Hirschenauer and Albrecht Weber. München: R. Oldenbourg Verlag, 1971.

330. Uhlig, G. *Autor, Werk und Kritik. Inhaltsangaben. Kritiken und Textproben für den Literaturunterricht*. Vol. I. München: Hueber, 1969, pp. 68-94.

331. Van der Will, Wilfried. "Die Blechtrommel," *Pikaro heute*. Stuttgart: W. Kohlhammer Verlag, 1967, pp. 63-69.

332. *Verleihung des Georg Büchner Preises 1965 an Günter Grass: Festrede und Laudatio*. Neuwied: Luchterhand, 1965.

333. Wagenbach, Klaus. "Günter Grass," *Schriftsteller der Gegenwart*. Ed. Klaus Nonnemann. Olten and Freiburg im Breisgau: Walter Verlag, 1963, pp. 118-126.

334. Weber, Werner. "Günter Grass: 'Brandmauern'," *Tagebuch eines Lesers*. Freiburg im Breisgau: Walter Verlag, 1965, pp. 88-92.

335. —————. "örtlich betäubt," *Forderungen*. Freiburg im Breisgau: Walter Verlag, 1970, pp. 179-185.

336. Wegener, Adolph. "Günter Grass, der realistische Zauberlehrling," *Helen Adolf Festschrift*. Eds. Sheema Z. Buehne, James L. Hodge, and Lucille B. Pinto. New York: Ungar, 1968, pp. 285-298.

337. Wieser, Theodor. *Günter Grass*. Neuwied: Luchterhand, 1968.

338. Willson, A. Leslie, ed. *A Günter Grass Symposium*. Austin: The University of Texas Press, 1971.

339. Yates, Norris W. *Günter Grass: A Critical Essay*. Grand Rapids, Michigan: William B. Eerdmans Publishing Company, 1967.

340. Zimmermann, W. "Günter Grass: *Katz und Maus*," *Deutsche Prosadichtungen unseres Jahrhunderts*. Vol. II, 1969, pp. 267-300.

JOURNAL AND NEWSPAPER ARTICLES

341. Ahlsson, Lars-Eric. "Zur Wortbildung bei Günter Grass. Das zusammengesetzte Adjektiv," *Studia neophilologus*, XLIII (1971), 180-197.

342. Aick, Gerhard. "Günter Grass's new play: What's good, what isn't," *Atlas*, XVIII, 1 (July, 1969), 56-57. (D)

343. Arimond, C. "Hundejahre," *Extension*, LX (August, 1965), 48. (Rev)

344. Arnold, Fritz. "Aus der Zwergperspektive," *Augsburger Allgemeine* (December 5/6, 1959). (Bt)

345. Arnold, Heinz Ludwig. "Grass-Kritiker," *Text und Kritik*, I, 1 (1965), 32-36.

346. —————. "Grosses Ja und Kleines Nein," *Frankfurter Rundschau* (March 8, 1969).

347. —————. "Die unpädagogische Provinz des Günter Grass," *Text und Kritik*, I, 1 (1965), 13-15.

348. Arp, Jochen. "Günter Grass reitet für die SPD," *Deutsche National- und Soldaten-Zeitung* München (April 11, 1969).

349. Ascherson, Neal. "The Lonely German," *Observer* (July 26, 1970), p. 7.

350. —————. "The Man who Bangs the Drum for Moderation," *Observer* (April 18, 1971), p. 10.

351. Augstein, Rudolf. "William Shakespeare, Bert Brecht, Günter Grass—Die Plebejer proben den Aufstand," *Der Spiegel*, XX, 5 (January 24, 1966), 83-87. (Pl)

352. B., W. "Grass spielt Katz und Maus," *Nürnberger Nachrichten* (November 17, 1961). (KuM)

353. Baecker, Sigurd. "Vier Akte Zaudern," *Vorwärts* (February 16, 1966). (Pl)

354. Bänziger, Hans. "Zwergengetrommel zwischen Ost und West," *Die Tat* (January 9, 1960). (Bt)

355. Baiè, Bernhard. "Trommelei auf Blech," *Recklinghäuser Zeitung* (February 6, 1960). (Bt)

356. Baier, Lothar. "Gedicht als Schnitt durch die Wirklichkeit, zur Lyrik von Günter Grass," *Text und Kritik*, I, 1 (1965), 9-12.

357. —————. "Weder ganz noch gar," *Text und Kritik*, I, 1 (1965), 28-30.

358. Bance, A. F. "The Enigma of Oskar in Grass' *Blechtrommel*," *Seminar: A Journal of Germanic Studies*, III (Spring, 1967), 147-156. (Bt)

359. Baranowski, W. "Das Holz aus dem man Helden schnitzt," *Das andere Deutschland* (January, 1962), p. 2. (KuM)

360. Baring, Arnulf. "Kipphardt, Grass, und die SPD," *Die Zeit*, No. 26 (June 29, 1971), pp. 9 & 10.

361. Baroth, Hans Dieter. "Das Ärgernis Grass," *Westfälische Rundschau*, Dortmund (September 1, 1963).

362. Barthel, Walter. "Das höhere Blech des Blechtrommlers," *Berliner Extradienst* (January 23, 1971).

363. Batt, Kurt. "Groteske und Parabel," *Neue Deutsche Literatur*, XII, 7 (1964), 57-75. (Hj)

364. Bauer, Helmuth. "Ein Goethe für unsere Tage. Interview mit Günter Grass," *Donau-Kurier* (March 15, 1969).

365. Bauer, Leo. "Ich bin Sozialdemokrat, weil ich ohne Furcht leben will. Gespräch mit Günter Grass" *Die Neue Gesellschaft*, Bad Godesberg, No. 2 (1971).

366. Bauke, Joseph P. "A Talk with Günter Grass," *New York Times Book Review*, LXIX, 22 (May 31, 1964), 16.

367. —————. "To be different in Danzig," *Saturday Review*, XLVI, 31 (August 10, 1963), 28.

368. Baukloh, Friedhelm. "Grass-Ruhm," *Deutsche Volkszeitung*, Düsseldorf (May 15, 1970).

369. Baumgart, Reinhard. "Günter Grass: *Katz und Maus*," *Neue Deutsche Hefte*, VIII (January, 1962). (KuM)

370. —————. "Kleinbürgertum und Realismus," *Neue Rundschau*, LXXV, 4 (1966), 650. (Pl)

371. —————. "Mustermesse deutsche Prosa," *Süddeutsche Zeitung*, München (July 6, 1963), p. 5.

372. _____. "Plebejer-Spätlese," *Neue Rundschau*, LXXVII, 2 (1966), 335. (Pl)

373. _____. "Unser Mann in Berlin?" *Süddeutsche Zeitung*, München (June 8/9, 1968).

374. Bayer, Hans. "Vielleicht ein politisches Tagebuch. Der Autor der *Blechtrommel* äussert sich über seinen Standort nach dem Wahlkampf," *Stuttgarter Nachrichten* (November 21, 1969).

375. Becker, Hellmut. "Lehrer und Schüler in Günter Grass' *örtlich betäubt*," *Neue Sammlung*, IX (1969), 503-510. (öb)

376. _____. "Lehrer und Schüler—neu gesehen," *Die Zeit*, No. 8 (February 25, 1969), p. 11. (öb)

377. Becker, Rolf. "Mässig mit Malzbonbons," *Der Spiegel*, XXIII, 33 (August 11, 1969), 102-103. (öb)

378. Beer, K. W. "Grass und die Folgen," *Die Politische Meinung*, X, 108 (1965), 8-11.

379. Behrend, Johanna E. "Auf der Suche nach dem Adamsapfel. Der Erzähler Pilenz in Günter Grass' Novelle *Katz und Maus*," *Germanisch-romanische Monatsschrift*, XIX (1969), 313-326. (KuM)

380. _____. "Die Ausweglosigkeit der menschlichen Natur. Eine Interpretation von Günter Grass' *Katz und Maus*," *Zeitschrift für deutsche Philologie*, LXXXVII (1968), 546-562. (KuM)

381. "Bei Grass abgeschaltet," *Bayern-Kurier*, München (December 6, 1969).

382. Bentley, Eric. "In Bahnhof Friedrichsstrasse," *Partisan Review*, XXXIII, 1 (Winter, 1966), 97-109.

383. Berger, Friedrich. "Es lohnt doch mit Grass den Aufstand zu proben," *Kölner Stadtanzeiger* (January 16, 1967), p. 10. (Pl)

384. "Berliner SPD distanziert sich von Grass," *Frankfurter Allgemeine Zeitung* (July 26, 1965).

385. "Bestseller auf Vorschuss," *Konkret* (September, 1963), p. 30. (Hj)

386. "Bild eines Bestsellerautors," *Bonner Generalanzeiger* (October 18, 1963), p. 7.

387. Blaha, Paul. "Glanz und Elend des Intellektuellen," *Der Kurier*, Wien (May 16, 1966), p. 12. (Pl)

388. "Der Blick von der Irrenanstalt," *Neophilologus*, LI, 1 (January, 1967), 42. (Bt)

389. Blöcker, Günter. "Im Zeichen des Hundes," *Frankfurter Allgemeine Zeitung*, Literaturblatt (September 14, 1963). (Hj)

390. _____. "Rückkehr zur Nabelschnur," *Frankfurter Allgemeine Zeitung*, Literaturblatt (November 28, 1959). (Bt)

391. _____. "Wir alle sind Schnecken," *Süddeutsche Zeitung*, München (August 26, 1972). (TS)

392. Blomster, Wesley V. "The Demonic in History: Thomas Mann and Günter Grass," *Contemporary Literature*, X, 1 (Winter, 1969), 73-84. (Hj)

393. _____. "The Documentation of a Novel: Otto Weininger and *Hundejahre* by Günter Grass," *Monatshefte*, LXI, 2 (Summer, 1969), 122-138. (Hj)

394. _____. "Oskar at the Zoppoter Waldoper," *Modern Language Notes*, LXXXIV, 3 (April, 1969), 467-472. (Bt)

395. Boa, Elizabeth. "Günter Grass and the German Gremlin." *German Life and Letters*, XXIII (January, 1970), 144-151.

396. Bock, Hans Bertram. "Günter Grass auf 'Es-Pe-De-Wahl-Tournee' in Würzburg und Nürnberg trommelte für Willy," *Abendzeitung*, München (July 15, 1965).

397. ───────. "Stützen der Gesellschaft," *Abendzeitung/8-Uhr-Blatt*, Nürnberg/München (February 22, 1968).

398. Böschenstein, Bernhard. "Günter Grass als Nachfolger Jean Pauls und Döblins," *Jahrbuch der Jean-Paul-Gesellschaft*, VI (1971), 86-101.

399. Botsford, Keith. "Günter Grass is a Different Drummer," *New York Times Magazine* (May 8, 1966), pp. 28ff.

400. Bourée, Manfred. "Das Okular des Günter Grass," *Echo der Zeit* (November 18, 1962).

401. Braem, Helmut M. "Narr mit dem Janusgesicht," *Stuttgarter Zeitung* (October 24, 1959). (Bt)

402. Brandell, Gunnar. "Günter Grass," *Svenska Dagbladet* (January 20, 1964). (Hj)

403. Brown, Thomas K. "*Die Plebejer* and Brecht: An Interview with Günter Grass," *Monatshefte*, LXV, 1 (Spring, 1973), 5-13. (Pl)

404. Bruce, James C. "Equivocating Narrator in *Katz und Maus*," *Monatshefte*, LVIII, 2 (Summer, 1966), 139-151. (KuM)

405. ───────. "The Motif of Failure and the Act of Narrating in Günter Grass' *örtlich betäubt*," *Modern Fiction Studies*, XVII, 1 (Spring, 1971), 61-80. (öb)

406. Brügge, Peter. "Wählerdiskussion mit Günter Grass," *Der Spiegel*, XX, 48 (November 21, 1966), 41.

407. ───────. "Zischoman, Zischoplex, Zischophil," *Der Spiegel*, XIX, 31 (July 28, 1965).

408. Brunelli, Vittorio. "Autopsy of an Insurrection," *Atlas*, XI, 4 (April, 1966), 249-250. (Pl)

409. Bucerius, Gerd. "Wogegen sie kämpfen, das wissen sie," *Die Zeit*, No. 12 (March 15, 1968).

410. Budzinski, Klaus. "Der Poet in der Manege," *Abendzeitung*, München (July 21, 1965).

411. "Bücher: demnächst in Deutschland," *Der Spiegel*, XXIII, 5 (January 27, 1969), 114. (öb)

412. Buèges, Jean. "Telégrammes-Livres," *Paris Match,* No. 864 (October 30, 1965).

413. Busch, Günther. "Spektakel und Desillusionierung," *Panorama* (April, 1960). (Bt)

414. —————. "Spektakel und Desillusionierung," *Wort in der Zeit*, VI, 2 (1960), 58-59. (Bt)

415. Carlsson, Anni. "Der Roman als Anschauungsform der Epoche. Bemerkungen zu Thomas Mann und Günter Grass," *Neue Zürcher Zeitung*, No. 321 (November 21, 1964), p. 23.

416. Carpelan, Bo. "Günter Grass," *Hufstudstadtsbladet*, Helsinki (December 28, 1962). (Bt)

417. —————. "Günter Grass," *Hufstudstadtsbladet*, Helsinki (December 28, 1962). (KuM)

418. Castein, Hanne. "Grass verärgert London," *Die Zeit*, No. 33 (August 18, 1970), p. 13. (Pl)

419. Church, M. *et al.* "Five Modern German Novelists: A Bibliography (1960-1970)," *Modern Fiction Studies*, XVII, 1 (Spring, 1971), 140-141.

420. Clements, R. J. "European Literary Scene," *Saturday Review*, LII, 43 (December 6, 1969), 40.

421. Cook, Bruce. "Young Germans Rant at Sins of the Fathers," *The National Observer*, IX, 42 (October 19, 1970), 22.

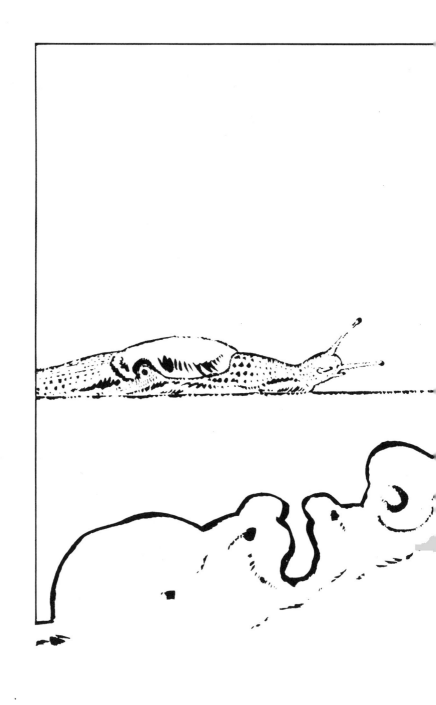

Günter Grass
From the Diary
of a Snail

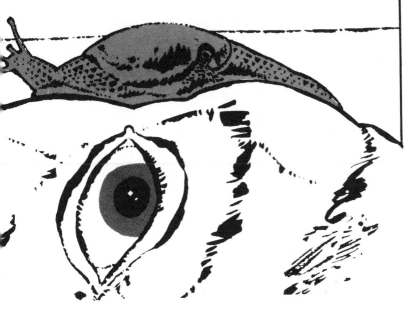

422. Cunliffe, W. Gordon. "Aspects of the Absurd in Günter Grass," *Wisconsin Studies in Contemporary Literature*, VII, 3 (Autumn, 1966), 310-327.

423. —————. "Grass and the Denial of Drama," *Dimension*, III, Special Issue (1970), 64-74.

424. —————. "Günter Grass: *Katz und Maus*," *Studies in Short Fiction*, III, 2 (Winter, 1966), 174-185. (KuM)

425. Cysarz, Herbert. "Verdient unsere Zeit diesen Bestseller?" *Deutsche National-Zeitung und Soldatenzeitung*, München (November 15, 1963). (KuM)

426. Dahne, Gerhard. "Wer ist Katz und wer ist Maus?" *Neue Deutsche Literatur*, XIII (November, 1965). (KuM)

427. "Das sagt die CDU zu Grass:" *Flugblatt der CDU*, Cloppenburg (September 17, 1965).

428. Deen, Rosemary F. "Günter Grass: Selected Poems," *Commonweal*, LXXXIV, 21 (September 16, 1966), 594.

429. Delmas, Eugene. "Ein deutsches Trauerspiel um Bertold Brecht," *Frankfurter Neue Presse* (January 18, 1966). (Pl)

430. "The Dentist's Chair as an Allegory of Life," *Time*, XCV, 15 (April 13, 1970), 68-79. (öb)

431. "Der Dichter mit der Dreckschleuder," *BILD*, Berlin (September 27, 1969).

432. "Der Dichter und die Politik," *Hamburger Abendblatt* (July 7, 1965)

433. Dixon, Christa K. "Ernst Barlach: *Die Sündflut* und Günter Grass: *Hochwasser*. Ein Beitrag zum Vergleich," *The German Quarterly*, XLIV, 3 (May, 1971), 360-371. (Hw)

434. Dobozy, Imre. "Der Irrtum des Günter Grass," *Neues Deutschland*, East Berlin (October 13, 1969).

435. Dönhoff, Marion Gräfin. "Der Versuch, ohne Utopie zu leben," *Die Zeit*, No. 8 (February 25, 1969), p. 11. (D)

436. Dörrlamm, Rolf. "Wer hat Angst vor Günter Grass?" *PUBLIK*, Frankfurt (January 17, 1969).

437. "Dog Years," *London Times Literary Supplement* (September 28, 1968). (Hj)

438. "Dogs and the Deflation of Demons," *London Times Literary Supplement* (September 27, 1963). p. 728. (Hj)

439. Dornheim, Alfredo. "Ernst Kreuder y Günter Grass," *Boletín de Estudios Germánicos*, VI (September, 1967), 125-145.

440. Drath, Viola Herms. "Der Stille Intellektuelle," *Madame* (March, 1967), p. 6.

441. Drehnaus, Karl Heinz. "Sind die Deutschen keine Nation?" *Vorwärts*, Bonn (July 6, 1967).

442. Droste, Dietrich. "Gruppenarbeit als Mittel der Erschliessung umfangreicher Romane: Grimmelshausens *Abenteuerlicher Simplicius Simplicissimus* und Grass' *Die Blechtrommel*," *Der Deutschunterricht*, XXI, 6 (1969), 101-115. (Bt)

443. "Drum of Neutrality," *London Times Literary Supplement* (October 5, 1962), p. 776. (Bt)

444. Durzak, Manfred. "örtlich betäubt," *Basis*, I (1970), 224-237. (Rev. öb)

445. _____. "Plädoyer für eine Rezeptionssästhetik. Anmerkungen zur deutschen und amerikanischen Literaturkritik am Beispiel von Günter Grass' *örtlich betaubt*," *Akzente*, No. 18 (1971), pp. 487-504. (öb)

446. E. K. "Onkel, Onkel," *Stuttgarter Zeitung* (March 16, 1966). (OO)

447. Edschmid, Kasimir. "Rede auf den Preisträger," *Deutsche Akademie für Sprache und Dichtung, Darmstadt, Jahrbuch* (1965), pp. 82-91.

448. Eichholz, Armin. "Dabeisein oder nicht dabeisein," *Münchner Merkur* (January 17, 1966). (Pl)

449. Eimers, Enno W. "Ein Schelmenroman unsere Tage—voll innerer Gesichte," *Der Kurier*, Berlin (November 28, 1959). (Bt)

450. "Ein Staat ist noch kein Vaterland," *Christ und Welt*, No. 6 (1966), pp. 19-20.

451. Eitel, Klaus, "Wir brauchen härtere Provokateure," *Darmstädter Echo* (October 11, 1965).

452. Elliott, John R. "The Cankered Muse of Günter Grass," *Dimension*, I, 1 (1968), 516-523. (Bt)

453. Elsom, John. "The English prepare Günter Grass," *London Magazine*, X, 7 (October, 1970), 81-86.

454. Engert, Jürgen. "Gespaltene Toleranz," *Der Abend*, Berlin (June 1, 1971).

455. _____. "Ich bin zu realistisch," *Christ und Welt* (July 3, 1970).

456. _____. "Lästige Wahlhelfer," *Christ und Welt* (May 28, 1965).

457. Enright, D. J. "Casting out Demons: *Dog Years*," *New York Review of Books*, IV, 9 (June 3, 1965), 8-10. (Hj)

458. Enzensberger, Hans Magnus. "Günter Grass: *Hundejahre*," *Der Spiegel*, XVII, 36 (September 2, 1963), 42. (Hj)

459. _____. "Trommelt weiter," *Frankfurter Hefte* (December, 1961). (KuM)

460. Esser, Josef. "Grass täuscht sich in SPD und Demokratie," *Die Zeit*, No. 8 (February 25, 1969), p. 20.

461. Ewen, Frederic. "Alas, Poor Bertold Brecht," *Nation*, CCIV, 7 (February 13, 1967), 213-124. (Rev. Pl)

462. Eysen, Jürgen. "Günter Grass: Katz und Maus," *Bücherei und Bildung, II* (February, 1962), 75. (KuM)

463. _____. F. "Möorder und sein Publikum," *Göttinger Presse* (June 1, 1961). (00)

464. F., K. "Dreht euch nicht um! Der Knirscher geht um," *Schwäbische Donauzeitung*, Ulm (August 21, 1963). (Hj)

465. _____. "Der Grosse Mahlke und das Dingslamdei," *Schwäbische Donauzeitung*, Ulm (October 5, 1961). (KuM)

466. Feldman, B. "Günter Grass: Four Plays," *Denver Quarterly*, II, 1 (Spring, 1967), 158.

467. Fickert, Kurt J. "The Use of Ambiguity in *Cat and Mouse*," *The German Quarterly*, XLIV, 3 (May, 1971), 372-378. (KuM)

468. Fiedler, Werner. "Der Rest ein dunkles Sösschen," *Der Tag*, Berlin (February 18, 1961). (BK)

469. Fiel, Anne-Marie and Philippe Ganier-Raymond, eds. *"L'Express* va plus loin avec Günter sic Grass," *L'Express*, No. 1057 (October 11-17, 1971), pp. 84-90.

470. Finges, Eva. "Grass Roots," *Guardian* (November 12, 1965), p. 11.

471. Fink, Humbert. "Dennoch mehr als ein Abfallprodukt," *Die Presse*, Wien (November 19, 1961). (KuM)

472. _____. "Ein Zwerg Haut auf die Trommel," *Heute*, Wien (December 12, 1959). (Bt)

473. Firgau, Walter. "Prozess um Ziesels Grass-Beschimpfung," *Süddeutsche Zeitung*, München (October 24, 1968).

474. Fischer, Gerd. "Vom Dingslamdei," *Neue Rhein-Zeitung*, Essen (October 7, 1961). (KuM)

475. Fischer, Heinz. "Excercismo de la lengua alemana," *Filología Moderna*, VI (1966), 29-42.

476. _____. "Sprachliche Tendenzen bei Heinrich Böll und Günter Grass," *The German Quarterly*, XL, 3 (May, 1967), 372-383.

477. Flach, Karl-Hermann. "Das ist nicht nur eine griechische Affäre. Die Militärdiktatur in Athen geht alle Europäer an," *Frankfurter Rundschau* (December 10, 1969).

478. Fliscar, Fritz. "Input-Interview," *Input*, No. 12 (1970).

479. Forster, Leonard. "Günter Grass," *University of Toronto Quarterly*, XXXVIII, 1 (October 1, 1968), 1-16.

480. Frank-Planitz, Ulrich. "Schwarzer Mann Grass," *Deutsche Zeitung/Christ und Welt*, Stuttgart (June 18, 1971).

481. Freedman, Ralph. "The Poet's Dilemma: The Narrative Worlds of Günter Grass," *Dimension*, III, Special Issue (1970), 50-63.

482. French, Philip. "Gone to Grass," *New Statesman* (February 16, 1968). (Pl)

483. Fricke, Dieter. "Herr Grass, sprengende Schnecken und das west-deutsche Hotel-frühstück," *Volkswacht,* East Berlin (August 7, 1970).

484. Fried, Erich. "Ist Ausgefragt fragwürdig?" *Konkret* (July, 1967). (Au)

485. _____. "Protestgedichte gegen Protestgedichte," *Die Zeit*, No. 33 (August 15, 1967), p. 20.

486. Friedrichsmeyer, Erhard M. "Aspects of Myth, Parody, and Obscenity in Grass' *Die Blechtrommel*

and *Katz und Maus*," *The Germanic Review*, XL, 3 (May, 1965), 240-249. (Bt, KuM) .

487. _____. "The Dogmatism of Pain: *Local Anaesthetic*," *Dimension*, III, Special Issue (1970), 36-49. (öb)

488. Frisch, Max, "Grass als Redner," *Die Zeit*, No. 38 (September 21, 1965), p. 16.

489. Fulton, Edythe K. "Günter Grass' Cat and Mouse Obsession and Life," *Forum*, Houston, VII, 2 (1969), 26-31. (KuM)

490. Furian, Heinz J. "Aufstand gegen die Meinungsdiktatur," *Das Andere Deutschland*, Hannover (October 1, 1967).

490a. Fuz, George C. "Morderstwo sadowe popelnione w 1939 r.na obroncach poczty polskiej w Wolnym Miescie Gdansku," *Panstwo i Prawo*, Polish Academy of Sciences, Warsaw (June, 1972).

491. G.,E. "Ein Zauberer trommelt ein Märchen," *Arbeiterzeitung*, Wien (January 6, 1960). (Bt)

492. "Galerie der Buhmänner. Gespräch mit Günter Grass," *Kontraste, Freiburg (January/February, 1967)*.

493. Garrott, Thomas J. "Oskars Empfang in England," *Die Zeit*, No. 43 (October 23, 1962), p. 15 (Bt)

494. Gast, Simon, "Die Literarischen Kometen," *Westermanns Monatshefte*, CVIII, 12 (December, 1967), 68-71.

495. Geerdts, Hans Jürgen, Peter Gugisch, Gerhard Kasper, Rudolf Schmidt. "Zur Problematik der kritischoppositionellen Literatur in Westdeutschland," *Wissenschaftliche Zeitschrift* der *Ernst-Moritz-Arndt-Universität Griefswald*, IX, 4/5 (1959/1960), 357-368.

496. "Gegen die Anmassung des Bürgers Grass," *Darmstädter Echo* (October 11, 1965).

497. "Der Geist Stalins über Prag," *Abendzeitung/8-Uhr-Blatt,* München (August 22, 1968).

498. Gelly, Alexander. "Art and Reality in *Die Blechtrommel,*" *Forum for Modern Language Studies,* University of St. Andrews, Scotland, III (1967), 115-125. (Bt)

499. Giegold, Heinrich. "Der unbequeme, offene Günter Grass. Frankenpost-Interview mit einem Schriftsteller, der Demokratie ernst nimmt," *Frankenpost,* Hof (December 24,1968).

500. Gilman, Richard. "Spoiling the Broth," *Newsweek,* LXIX, 6 (February 6, 1967), 106. (Rev, BK)

501. "Gipfel des Grass-Ruhms," *Unsere Zeitung,* Bremen, V, 160 (May, 1970), 2.

502. Gittleman, Sol. "Günter Grass: Notes on the Theology of the Absurd," *The Crane Review,*Tufts University, VIII (1965), 32-35.

503. Grack, Günter. "Fünf Gänge, die nicht sättigen," *Der Tagesspiegel,* Berlin (February 18,1961). (BK)

504. "Grass and his Nation's Burdens," *London Times Literary Supplement* (September 25, 1966), pp. 1077-1078.

505. "Grass at the Roots," *Time,* XCIV, 10 (September 5, 1969), 24 & 29.

506. "Grass—Aufstand der Plebejer," *Der Spiegel,* XIX, 51 (December 13, 1965), 127-128. (Pl)

507. "Grass contra Springer," *Die Zeit,* No. 40 (October 3, 1967), pp. 9-10.

508. "Grass-Dingslamdei," *Der Spiegel,* XV, 42 (October 9, 1961), 88-91. (KuM)

509. "Grass empfiehlt Prager Modell. Auszüge aus dem Interview, das Günter Grass am 27. Juni 1968 dem Jugendfunk von 'Radio Prag'˙gegeben hat," *Süddeutsche Zeitung,* München (June 29, 1968).

510. "Grass gegen Brecht," *Atlas,* IX, 4 (April, 1965), 249. (Pl)

511. "Grass, Günter, Walter Höllerer, and Walter Hasenclever: Writers in Berlin," *Atlantic,* CCXII, 6 (December, 1963), 110-113.

512. "Grass-Interview," *Die Glocke,* Schülerzeitung der Schillerschule Hannover, XI, 49 (December, 1967).

513. "Grass-Kritik: Wallerands Weh," *Der Spiegel,* XVI, 9 (February 19,1962), 68-69.

514. "Grass: Not des Bürgers," *Der Spiegel,* XXI, 42 (October 9, 1967).

515. "Grass Premier—Die Bösen Köche," *Der Speigel,* XIV, 10 (February 29, 1960), 77-78, (BK)

516. "Grass Takes to the Stump." *America,* CXIII, 4 (July 24, 1965), 89.

517. "Grass und das Nationalgefühl," *Deutsche Wochenzeitung,* Hannover (December 9, 1967).

518. "Grass, Uwe Johnson Among Authors with new Works," *The Bulletin,* XVIII, 36 (October 20,1970), 280. (öb)

519. "Grass: Wähler braucht nicht unbedingt ein Parteibuch," *Hannoversche Presse* (July 24,1969).

520. "Grass: Wenn es nicht klappt—dann Opposition. Wer regiert mit wem?" *Abendzeitung/8-Uhr-Blatt,* München (October 1, 1969).

521. "Grass: Wiedervereinigung muss aus Sprachschatz gestrichen werden," *Abendzeitung*, München (May 30, 1967), p. 5.

522. "Grass wirbt für die FDP," *Abendzeitung*, München (February 28, 1967), p. 1.

523. "Grass: Zunge heraus," *Der Spiegel*, XVII, 36 (September 2, 1963), 64-69, 72-78. (Hj)

524. Grathoff, Dirk. "Schnittpunkte von Literatur und Politik. Günter Grass und die neuere deutsche Grass-Rezeption," *Basis*, I (1970), 134-152.

525. Gregor-Dellin, Martin. "Kein Ende des Spiels," *Süddeutsche Zeitung*, München (June 16/17, 1971).

526. Gröniger, Wolfgang. "Zeichen an der Wand," *Hochland* (December, 1959). (Bt)

527. Grüber, Heinrich, "Verantwortung für die Sicherung der Zukunft," *Bulletin der Bundesregierung*, Bonn (April 11, 1968).

528. Grunenberg, Nina. "Auf hohem Seil zwischen CDU und DKP," *Die Zeit*, No. 41 (October 12, 1971), p. 11.

529. —————. "Günter Grass an der SPD-Front," *Die Zeit*, No. 13 (April 1, 1969) p. 9.

530.. —————. "Leon, ein polnischer Student," *Die Zeit*, No. 52/1 (January 2, 1973), p. 11.

531. Grunfeld, Fred. "Drums along the Vistula," *Reporter*, XXVIII, 6 (March 14, 1963), 54-57. (Bt)

532. "Günter Grass," *Kultura*, Warsaw (June 26, 1966). (Hj)

533. "Günter Grass," *Schwäbische Zeitung*, Laupheim (September 27, 1969).

534. "Günter Grass," *Stern*, XXII, 41 (October 12, 1969), 9.

535. "Günter Grass entgegnet der Schaubühne," *Die Welt* (June 4, 1971).

536. "Günter Grass—Interview," *Retorte,* Schülerzeitung, Ludwigshafen (December, 1966).

537. "Günter Grass: Kalte Heimat," *Der Spiegel,* XXIV, 40 (September 28, 1970).

538. "Günter Grass Preis," *The German Quarterly,* XLIII, 2 (March, 1970), 329-330.

539. "Günter Grass' *Upright* [sic] Scores Washington Success," *The Bulletin,* Bonn, XX, 12 (March 28, 1972), 92. (D)

540. "Günter Grass zu seinem Misserfolg." *Stuttgarter Nachrichten* (March 10, 1969).

541. Günzel, Manfred. "Der Blechtrommler (Eine Parodie auf Günter Grass)," *Blätter und Bilder,* XII (1961), 79. (Bt)

542. "The Guilt of the Lambs," *Time,* LXXXI, 1 (January 4, 1963), 69ff.

543. Gutwillig, Robert. "Günter Grass," *New York Herald Tribune* (August 11, 1963). (KuM)

544. György, Walko. "Günter Grass és a botránkozok," *Nagyvilág,* VI, 6 (September 10, 1967), 825-827.

545. Habernoll, Kurt. "Unpolitisches Theater in politischer Kaschierung," *Vorwärts* (February 16, 1966), pp. 23-24. (Pl)

546 Härtling, Peter. "Gedichte zu Gelegenheiten," *Der Spiegel,* XXI, 29 (July 9, 1967), 37. (Au)

547. _____. "Von Langfuhr in die Scheuchengrube," *Der Monat,* XV, 180 (September, 1963), 62-68. (Hj)

548. Häsler. "Gespräch mit Günter Grass," *Ex Libris,* Zürich (May, 1969), pp. 11-25.

549. Häussermann, Bernhard. "Ein Buch, in dem es päsert und funkert," *Hannoversche Allgemeine* (September 7, 1963). (Hj)

550. Hahnl, Hans Heinz. "Auf dem Weg sur Zeitkritik, unserer Misere," *Arbeiterzeitung,* Wien (May 17, 1966). (Pl)

551. —————. "Der Neue Grass," *Die Zukunft,* Wien (September, 1963). (Hj)

552. Hamburger, Michael. "Moralist and Jester: The Poetry of Günter Grass," *Dimension,* III, Special Issue (1970), 75-90.

553. Hamm, Peter. "Alles Schöne ist schief," *Twen,* Köln (July, 1967) p. 22. (Au)

554. —————. "Grass und seine Kritiker," *Der Spiegel,* XXII, 49 (December 2, 1968), 190-193. (öb)

555. —————. "Vergeblicher Versuch, einen Chef zu entmündigen," *Frankfurter Hefte,* XXI, 3 (March, 1966), 206-208. (Pl)

556. —————. "Verrückte Lehr-und Wanderjahre," *Du,* Zürich, XIX, 12 (December, 1959), 132-136. (Bt)

557. Hanson, William P. "Oskar, Rasputin, and Goethe," *Canadian Modern Language Review,* XX, 1 (1963), 29-32. (Bt)

558. Harrington, Michael. "Politics of Günter Grass," *Atlantic Monthly,* CCXXIII, 4 (April, 1969), 129-131.

559. Hartl, Edwin. "Weltschmerz, dentistisch behandelt. Zu dem Roman *örtlich betäubt* von Günter Grass," *Literatur und Kritik,* No. 57 (1971), pp. 433-435.(öb)

560. Hartlaub, Geno, "Wir, die wir übriggeblieben sind," *Sonntagsblatt,* Hamburg (January 1, 1967).

561. Hartmann, Rainer. "Ein Trauerspiel vom deutschen Trauerspiel," *Frankfurter Neue Presse* (July 11, 1966), p. 10. (Pl)

562. Hartung, Günter. "Bobrowski und Grass," *Weimarer Beiträge*, XVI, 8 (1970), 203-224.

563. Hartung, Rudolf. "Hundejahre," *Neue Rundschau*, LXXIV, 4 (1963), 652-658. (Hj)

564. ——————. "Porträt eines Kriegshelden," *Der Tagesspiegel*, Berlin (November 26, 1961). (KuM)

565. Hassner, Pierre. "Wie viele Deutschlands," *Die Zeit*, No. 5 (February 4, 1969), p. 9.

566. Hausen, Herbert. "Der Ladenhüter des Herrn Grass," *Welt am Sonntag*, Berlin (June 4, 1967).

567. Hayman, Ronald. "Two Interviews: André Malraux, Günter Grass," *Encounter*, XXXV, 3 (September, 1970), 23-29.

568. ——————. "Underneath the Table," *London Times* (July 18, 1970), p. 7. (Bt)

569. Heidenreich, Gert. "Parteipropaganda als Dokumentation," *Die Zeit*, No. 25 (June 13, 1969).

570. Heinemann-Rufer, Ulrich. "Grass im Zuchthaus Tegel," *Die Zeit*, No. 40 (October 10, 1967), p. 11.

571. Heise, Hans-Jürgen. "Zwischen Politik und Literatur," *Die Tat*, Zürich (July 15, 1967). (Au)

572. Heissenbüttel, Helmut. "Und es kam Uwe Johnson," *Deutsche Zeitung*, Köln (November 10, 1960). (Gruppe 47)

573. Hensel, Georg. "Blechgetrommel um Günter Grass," *Darmstädter Echo* (September 24, 1965).

574. ——————. "Nicht nur von der Maus gefressen," *Darmstädter Echo* (November 18, 1961). (KuM)

575. Hepp, Marcel. "Neue Hundejahre," *Bayern-Kurier*, München (June 3, 1967).

576. —————. "Unangenehm für Grass," *Bayern-Kurier,*München (January 25, 1969).

577. Herburger, Günter. "Überlebensgross Herr Grass," *Die Zeit*, No. 23 (June 8, 1971), p. 9.

578. Herchenröder, Jan. "Ein Trommelfeuer von Einfällen," *Die Andere Zeitung,* Hamburg (March, 1960). (Bt)

579. —————. "Das schlimme Gleichnis von den Hundejahren," *Abendpost*, Frankfurt am Main (August 17, 1963). (Hj)

580. Hermann, Kai. "Wahlhelfer Grass," *Die Zeit,* No. 28 (July 8, 1965).

581. Hermlin, Stephan, *et al.* "Antworten aus der DDR," *Sonntag*, East Berlin (August 27, 1961).

582. Herms, Uwe. "Heute back ich, morgen brau ich, übermorgen...," *Stuttgarter Zeitung* (April 8, 1967), p. 19. (Au)

583. Herrmann, Walter M. "Schuldbewusst klage ich euch an!" *Hamburger Abendblatt* (January 5, 1968). (Pl)

584. Hewes, Henry. "Grass on Brecht," *Saturday Review*, LI, 37 (September 14, 1968), 117. (Pl)

585. —————. "Uptight," *Saturday Review*, LV, 21 (May 20, 1972), 63. (D)

586. Hildebrandt, Dieter. "Abendliches Gespräch mit einem von der Schaubühne verachteten Menschen," *PUBLIK*, Frankfurt (July 2, 1971).

587. —————. "Brecht und der Rasen," *Frankfurter Allgemeine Zeitung* (January 17, 1966). (Pl)

588. —————. "Günter Grass—der ernüchterte Orpheus," *Süddeutsche Zeitung,* München (May 25, 1968).

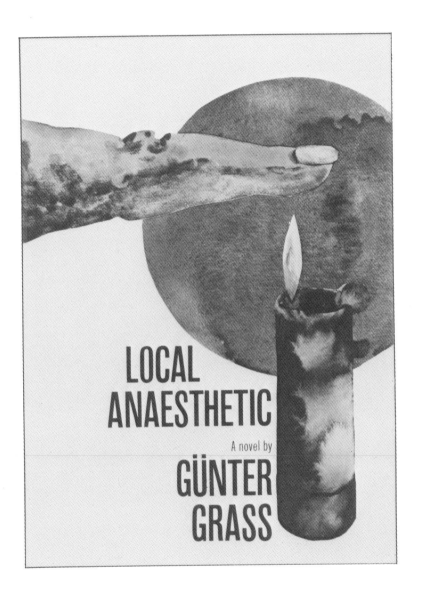

LOCAL
ANAESTHETIC

A novel by

GÜNTER
GRASS

[Item no. 179]

589. Hill, W. "Hundejahre," *Best*, XXV (June 1, 1965), 116. (Rev, Hj)

590. Hinderer, Walter. "Das waren noch Zeiten," *Die Zeit*, No. 20 (May 23, 1972), p. 12.

591. Hochmann, Sandra. "The Tin Drum," *The Village Voice*, New York (March 14, 1963). (Bt)

592. Höck, Wilhelm. "Der vorläufig abgerissene Faden. Günter Grass und das Dilemma des Erzählens," *Hochland*, LXI (1969), 558-563.

593. Höfer, Werner. "Nicht hinter Utopien herjagen," *Die Zeit*, No. 27 (June 28, 1968).

594. Höller, Franz. "Das Kraftgenie aus Danzig." *Ost-West-Kurier*, Frankfurt am Main (October, 1961). (KuM)

595. Höllerer, Walter. "Letter from Germany," *Evergreen Review*, IV, 15 (November/December 1960), 135-138.

596. —————. "Roman in Kreuzfeuer," *Berliner Tagesspiegel* (December 20, 1959). (Bt)

597. Höppner, Hans. "Die Rotmacher," *Spandauer Volksblatt*, Berlin (June 6, 1971).

598. Hoffman, Jens. "Grass und der Georg-Büchner Preis," *Christ und Welt*, XVIII, 42 (1965), 25.

599. Hohoff, Curt. "Die Welt der Vogelscheuchen," *Rheinischer Merkur*, Köln, No. 44 (November 15, 1963). (Hj)

600. Holthusen, Hans Egon. "Günter Grass als politischer Autor," *Der Monat*, XVIII, 216 (September, 1966), 66-81.

601. Honsza, Norbert. "Günter Grass und kein Ende?" *Annali Instituto Universitario Orientale, Napoli, Sezione Germanica* IX (1966), 177-187.

602. Hornung, Peter. "Die Gruppe, die keine Gruppe ist," *Tages-Anzeiger*, Regensburg (May, 1955), p. 8. (Gruppe 47)

603. —————. "Oskar Matzerath—Trommler und Gotteslästerer," *Deutsche Tagespost*, Würzburg (November 23, 1959), p. 3. (Bt)

604. —————. "Was man erlebt, wenn man zu jungen Dichtern fährt," *Neue Presse*, Passau (November 16, 1956). (Gruppe 47)

605. Horst, Karl August. "Ferne Trommelschläge," *Merkur*, XV, 12 (December, 1961), 1197-1198. (KuM)

606. —————. "Heimsuche," *Merkur,* XIII, 12 December, 1959), 1191-1195. (Bt)

607. —————. "Die Vogelscheuchen des Günter Grass," *Merkur*, XVII, 10 (October, 1963), 1003-1008. (Hj)

608. Hudak, Adalbert, *et al.* "Mit Kurt Ziesel gegen Grass solidarisch," *Abendzeitung/8-Uhr-Blatt*, Nürnberg/München (February 22, 1968).

609. Hübner, Paul. "Grass kratzt am Brecht-Mythos," *Rheinische Post*, Duisburg (January 17, 1966). (Pl)

610. Humm/Loetscher, G. "Gepfiffen und getrommelt," *Die Weltwoche*, Zürich (January 22, 1960). (Bt)

611. Hunt, Albert. "Escaping to Freedom," *New Society* (August 6, 1970), pp. 252-253.

612. Husson, Albert. "Zweimal verhinderter Mord," *Theater Rundschau* (April, 1958). (00)

613. "Ich bleibe bei Hosen," *Epoca*, München (October, 1969).

614. "Ich will auch der SDP einiges zumuten," *Der Spiegel*, XIX, 31 (July 28, 1965).

615. Ide, Heinz. "Dialektisches Denken im Werk von Günter Grass," *Studium generale*, XXI (1968), 608-622.

616. Ignée, Wolfgang. "Die Wahrheit ist konkret," *Christ und Welt* (January 21, 1966). (Pl)

617. Ihlau, Olaf. "Grass: Die Studenten vor dem Verschleiss durch den SDS retten," *Neue Ruhr-Zeitung*, Essen (March 29, 1969).

618. "Im Widerspruch zur Politik der SPD," *Sozialdemokratischer Pressidienst*, Bonn (July 21, 1965).

619. "In der Sackgasse des Antikommunismus," *Der Morgen*, Berlin (January 21, 1966). (Pl)

620. Isbáşescu, Mihai. "Günter Grass şi forţa epicului," *Secolul XX*, XII, 5 (1969), 65-70.

621. Jaesrich, Hellmut. "Günter Grass, or Dragon Hunting," *Encounter*, XXXVII, 5 (November, 1971), 60-64.

622. Jahnke, Jürgen. "Günter Grass als Stückeschreiber," *Text und Kritik*, I, 1(1965), 25-27.

623. James, Norman. "The Fusion of Pirandello and Brecht in *Marat/Sade* and *The Plebeians Rehearse the Uprising*," *Educational Theatre Journal*, XXI, 4 (December, 1969), 426-438. (Pl).

624. Jappe, Georg. "Zwischen allen Stühlen," *Die Zeit*, No. 50 (December 15, 1970), p. 9.

625. Jenny, Urs. "Ein Hundetorso aus Kartoffelschalen," *Die Weltwoche*, Zürich (October 4, 1963), p. 16. (Hj)

626. _____. "Grass probt den Aufstand," *Süddeutsche Zeitung* (January 17, 1966). (Pl)

627. _____. "Im Vakuum heiter bleiben," *Die Weltwoche*, Zürich (May 19, 1967), p. 26. (Au)

628. _____. "Rettet nun Grass die Kammerspiele?" *Süddeutsche Zeitung*, München (June 14, 1971).

629. Jens, Walter. "Das Pandämonium des Günter Grass," *Die Zeit*, No. 36 (September 6, 1963), p. 17. (Hj)

630. Jensen, Jorgen Bonde. "Kunstner og engagement," *Vindrosen*, Copenhagen, XIII, 5 (1966), 44-58.

631. Jerde, C.D. "A Corridor of Pathos: Notes on the Fiction of Günter Grass," *Minnesota Review*, IV, 4 (Summer, 1964), 558-560.

632. Joppe, Jaap. "Günter Grass," *Rotterdamsch Nieuwsblad* (November 21, 1964). (Bt)

633. Jürgens, Martin. "Ausgefragt," *Neue Rundschau*, LXXVIII, 3 (1967), 484-490. (Rev, Au)

634. K. "Die Blechtrommel," *Unser Danzig*, Lübeck (May 20, 1960), p. 1. (Bt)

635. K., A. "Sprachmächtige Flucht aus der Verantwortung," *Neues Winterthurer Tageblatt* (December 5, 1959). (Bt)

636. K., F. "Ein Prosit der Geschmacklosigkeit," *Neues Österreich,* Wien (October 20, 1962). (00)

637. K., K. "Grass and Johnson in New York," *American-German Review*, XXXI, 5 (1964/1965), 35-37.

638. Kabel, Rainer. "Grotesk ist zugleich auch moralisch," *Vorwärts* (October 2, 1963). (Hj)

639. Kadritzke, Ulf. "Über die nicht angelesene Kritik," *frontal*, Bonn (November , 1968).

640. Kafka, Vladimir. "Günter Grasse album fantastických grotesek," *Svetová literatura,* X, 2 (1965), 200-223.

641. _____. "Psi roky Güntera Grasse a Nemeka," *Kaizui kultura,* Prague, I, 2 (1964), 66ff (Hj)

642. Kahl, Kurt. "Nicht Brecht ist der Chef," *Theater Heute*, XVII, 7 (July, 1966), 35-37. (Pl)

643. Kaiser, Carl Christian. "Günter Grass gibt zu denken," *Stuttgarter Zeitung*, No. 122 (May 31, 1967).

644. Kaiser, Joachim. "Böse Kinder bleiben siegreich" *Süddeutsche Zeitung*, München (February 14, 1962). (00)

645. _____. "Bremer Blechtrommel-Skandal," *Süddeutsche Zeitung*, München (December 31, 1959).

646. _____. "Der gelassene Grass," *Süddeutsche Zeitung*, München (April 27, 1967). (Au)

647. _____. "Grass überfördert seinen Hamlet," *Süddeutsche Zeitung*, München (April 27, 1967). (Pl)

648. _____. "Die Gruppe 47 lebt auf," *Süddeutsche Zeitung*, München (November 5, 1958). (Gruppe 47)

649. _____. "Günter Grass' Lokomotiven-Poesie," *Süddeutsche Zeitung*, München (February 23, 1960). (NzM)

650. _____. "Oskars getrommelte Bekenntnisse," *Süddeutsche Zeitung*, München (October 30, 1959). (Bt)

651. _____. "Politik, Theater-Politik, kein Theater," *Süddeutsche Zeitung*, München (May 19/20, 1971).

652. _____. "Die Unbefangenheit des Raubtiers," *Süddeutsche Zeitung*, München (October 7, 1961). (KuM)

653. _____. "Walter Materns Hundejahre," *Süddeutsche Zeitung*, München (September 21/22, 1963). (Hj)

654. ——————. "Wie einst die Gruppe 47," *Die Zeit*, No. 20 (May 20, 1969), p. 13. (Gruppe 47)

655. ——————. "Zehn Jahre Gruppe 47." *Frankfurter Allgemeine Zeitung* (October 2, 1957). (Gruppe 47)

656. Kant, Hermann. "Ein Solo in Blech," *Neue Deutsche Literatur*, VIII (May, 1960). (Bt)

657. Karasek, Hellmuth. "Ballade vom armen Günter Grass," *Die Zeit*, No. 26 (June 29, 1971), pp. 9 & 10.

658. ——————. "Günter Grass und die Narren," *Die Zeit*, No. 25 (June 11, 1971).

659. ——————. "Hand aufs Herz bei Günter Grass," *Die Zeit*, No. 8 (February 25, 1969), p. 11. (D)

660. ——————. "Der Knorpel am Hals," *Stuttgarter Zeitung*(November 11, 1961). (KuM)

661. ——————. "Örtlich anders Betäubt," *Die Zeit*, No. 22 (June 2, 1970), p. 9. (öb)

662. ——————. "Wozu das viele Theater?" *Die Zeit*, No. 7 (February 18, 1969), p. 9. (D)

663. ——————. "Zahn gezogen," *Die Zeit*, No. 36 (September 9, 1969), p. 11. (öb)

664. Karthaus, Ulrich. "*Katz und Maus* von Günter Grass: Eine politische Dichtung," *Der Deutschunterricht*, XXIII, 1 (1971), 74-85. (KuM)

665. "Katz und Maus mit *Katz und Maus*," *Deutsche Tagespost*, Würzburg (March 20, 1963).

666. Kaufmann, Harald. "Hundejahre und satirischer Weltuntergang," *Neue Zeit*, Graz (November 9, 1963). (Hj)

667. Kayser, Beate. "Grass überwuchert die Stadt Danzig," *Münchner Merkur* (October 21, 1961). (KuM)

668. "Keeping off the Grass,'' *London Times Literary Supplement* (September 30, 1965), pp. 859-860.

669. "Kein Wahlkontor," *Die Zeit*, No. 5 February 4, 1969), p. 2.

670. Kermauner, Taras. "Kajuh i Balanlić: Dua odnosa prema problemima vremena i smrti," *Knjizevna Istorija*, Belgrade, I (1968), 865-885. (KuM)

671. Kern, Erich. "Meuterei enttäuschter Jugend," *Deutsche Wochenzeitung*, Hannover (December 9, 1966).

672. Kersten, Hans Ulrich. "Grass versus Brecht," *Basler Nachrichten* (January 19, 1966). (Pl)

673. Kesting, Marianne. "Günter Grass als Dramatiker," *Welt und Wort*, XVIII, 9 (September, 1963), 270.

674. Kienzl, Florian. "Aufstand gegen die Brecht-Legende," *Die Presse*, Wien (January 18, 1966). (Pl)

675. Kipphardt, Heinar. "Grass als Kämpfer gegen linken Terror," *Süddeutsche Zeitung*, München (May 10, 1971).

676. Kirn, Richard. "Sein Zwerg haut auf die Trommel," *Frankfurter Neue Presse* (November 14, 1959), p. 36. (Bt)

677. Klein, Otto. "Die Grässlichen Hundejahre," *Das Deutsche Wort*, Köln (October 18, 1963). (Hj)

678. "Kleine und grosse Meinungsfreiheit," *Volksbote*, München (October 14, 1967).

679. Klinge, Reinhold. "*Die Blechtrommel* im Unterricht?" *Der Deutschunterricht*, XVIII, 2 (1966), 91-103. (Bt)

680. Klotz, Volker. "Ein deutsches Trauerspiel," *Frankfurter Rundschau* (January 17, 1966). (Pl)

681. Kluger, Richard. "Tumultuous Indictment of Man," *Harper's Magazine,* CCXXX, 1381 (June, 1965).

682. Klunker, Heinz. "Günter Grass und seine Kritiker," *Europäische Begegnung,* IV (1964), 466-469.

683. _____. "Ich und meine Rollen. Wirklichkeit und Roman, Literatur und Politik, ein Gespräch," *Deutsches Allgemeines Sonntagsblatt* (October 12, 1969).

684. _____. "Örtlich begrenzt," *Deutsches Allgemeines Sonntagsblatt,* Hamburg (September 7, 1969).

685. _____. "Unpathetisches Denkmal für Mahlke," *Europäische Begegnung* (June, 1962). (KuM)

686. Köhler, Otto. "Porträt eines Dichters," *Der Spiegel,* XXI, 42 (October 9, 1967).

687. "Können Schriftsteller streiken? Spiegel-Gespräch mit Dieter Lattman und Günter Grass über den Autoren-Verband," *Der Spiegel,* XXII, 47 (November 16, 1970).

688. Kopplin, Wolfgang. "Zu einem Gedicht von Günter Grass ('Schulpause')," *Welt und Wort,* XXV, 2 (February, 1970), 43-44.

689. Korn, Karl. "Epitaph für Mahlke," *Frankurter Allgemeine Zeitung* (October 7, 1961), p. 21. (KuM)

690. Kotschenreuther, Hellmut. "Der Intellektuelle in der Diktatur, " *Mannheimer Morgen* (January 17, 1966). (Pl)

691. _____. "Politik nicht vom Olymp herab. Der Autor berichtet von seinen Eindrücken in Israel," *Neue Ruhr-Zeitung,* Essen (April 8, 1967).

692. Kozarynowa, Zofia. "Günter Grass," *Wiadomski,* London (July 21, 1963). (Bt)

693. Krämer-Badoni, Rudolf. "Brennendes Brett vor dem Kopf," *Wiesbadener Kurier* (September 24, 1965).

694. Krättli, Anton. "Günter Grass und die deutsche Buchkritik," *Schweizer Monatshefte,* XLIX, 753-760.

695. Kraft, Peter. "Vergleiche und ähnliche Alleskleber," *Oberösterreichsche Nachrichten,* Linz (June 22, 1967). (Au)

696. Kraft, Werner. "Kleine Gedichte von Günter Grass," *Merkur,* XXIII (1969), 492-494.

697. Kramberg, Karl Heinz. "Das kommende Buch," *Das Schönste,* München (February, 1960). (Bt)

698. Kraus, Wolfgang. "Zweispältiger Eindruck eines überdurchschnittlichen Romans," *National-Zeitung,* Basel (December 19, 1959). (Bt)

699. Krauschner, Helga. "Wohin mit der Wut?" *Die Furche,* Wien (April 8, 1967). (Au)

700. Krauss, Erika. "Kiesinger und Beate—ein schönes Paar," *Hamburger Morgenpost* (April 25, 1969).

701. Kridel, Boris. "Günter Grass woos the Bonn Voters," *Observer* (September 7, 1969). p. 9.

702. Kriegel, Leonard. "Günter Grass' Tale of Men and Molars in a Mended Germany," *Commonweal,* XCII, 8 (May 8, 1970), 195-196. (öb)

703. Krolow, Karl. "Alles Schöne ist schief," *Hannoversche Allgemeine* (April 14, 1967). (Au)

704. —————. "Ist es nur ein Schelmenroman?" *Nekar Echo,* Heilbronn (November 21/22, 1959). (Bt)

705. Krüger, Horst. "Des Kanzlers Klage," *Die Zeit,* No. 12 (March 25, 1969), p. 11.

706. —————. "Kein Geschmack für Ort und Augenblick," *Die Zeit*, No. 34 (August 26, 1969), p. 12. (öb)

707. —————. "Ohne Macht und Mandat," *Die Zeit*, No. 27 (July 7, 1970), p. 8.

708. —————. Ritratto di Günter Grass," *Settanta*, No. 14/15 (1971), pp. 61-62.

709. —————. "Das Wappentier der Republik," *Die Zeit*, No. 17 (April 29, 1969), p. 11.

710. "Künstlerpech," *Sonntagsblatt Staats-Zeitung und Herold* (November 20/21, 1971), p. B10.

711. Kuhn, Heinrich. "Tagewache auf der Blechtrommel gerührt," *National-Zeitung*, Basel (July 18, 1965). (Bt)

712. Kunkel, Francis L. "Clowns and Saviors: Two Contemporary Novels," *Renascence*, XVIII (Fall, 1965), 40-44. (KuM)

713. Kurz, Paul K., S. J. "Die Gruppe 47: Bericht und Politik," *Stimmen der Zeit*, XCIII (1968), 318-332. (Gruppe 47)

714. —————. "*Hundejahre*. Beobachtungen zu einem zeitkritischen Roman," *Stimmen der Zeit*, LXXXIX, 173 (1963/1964), 107-120. (Hj)

715. —————. "Das verunsicherte Wappentier," *Stimmen der Zeit*, XCIV, 184 (December, 1969), 374-389. (D & öb)

716. —————. "Von und über Günter Grass: über neue literarische Erscheinungen," *Stimmen der Zeit*, XCIV, 183 (May 1969), 321-329.

717. —————. "*Windhühner, Ausgefragt*: Zur Lyrik von Günter Grass," *Stimmen der Zeit*, XCII, 9 (September, 1967), 167-181. (VW & Au)

718. "Die Länder-Idylle des Günter Grass," *Die Andere Zeitung*, Hamburg (June 8, 1967).

719. Langfelder, Paul. "Günter Grass," *Vîata Rominesca*, Bucarest (November, 1964). (Hj)

720. Lattmann, Dieter. "Aug um Auge, Wahn um Wahn" *Süddeutsche Zeitung,* München (June 12/13, 1971).

721. —————. "Geborgte Vergangenheit—verspätete Gegenwart. Wie jung sind junge deutsche Autoren?" *Welt der Literatur* (December 23, 1965), pp. 751-752.

722. "Der lautlose Rückzug der 13 Springer-Redakteure," *Frankfurter Rundschau* (January 29, 1970).

723. "Leaves of Grass," *Time*, LXXXVII, 13 (April 1, 1966), 103-104.

724. Leber, Hugo. "Der kaschubische Trommler," *Tagesanzeiger für Stadt und Kanton Zürich* (September 26, 1960). (Bt)

725. Lebeer, Irmelin. "Günter Grass: Pour l'ecrivain, s'engager signifie travailler," *La quinzaine litteraire*, Paris (October 15, 1969).

726. Laiser, Erwin. "Brecht, Grass, und der 17. Juni 1953," *Die Weltwoche*, Zürich (February 11, 1966). (Pl)

727. —————. "Gespräch über Deutschland," *Die Weltwoche*, Zürich (December 23, 1966).

728. Lenz, Michael. "Gedichte in Moll," *Westdeutsche Allgemeine*, Essen (June 3, 1967). (Au)

729. Leonhardt, Rudolf Walter. "Das Ende der Resignation," *Die Zeit*, No. 43 (October 31, 1972), pp. 9-10.

730. —————. "Die Sorgen des PEN," *Die Zeit*, No. 18 (May 6, 1969), p. 13.

731. Leroy R. "Günter Grass: *Die Blechtrommel*, Hugo Claus: *DeVerwondering*. Hasard ou intention?" *Revue des langues vivantes*, XXXV (1969), 597-608; XXXVI, 45-53. (Bt)

732. Liber, Ernst. "Snails and other fellows," *International Scala*, English edition, No. 4 (April, 1973), p. 40.

733. Lindroth, James R. "Out of Hitler's Kennel," *America*, CXII, 26 (June 26, 1965), 903. (Rev, Hj)

734. Linke, Rainer. "Wer kennt schon Günter Grass," *Realist*, Schülerzeitung, Augsburg (November, 1969).

735. Lörinc, Peter. "Günter Grass," *Magyar Szó*, Budapest (January, 1964). (Bt)

736. Loetscher, Hugo. "Günter Grass," *Du,* Zürich, CCXXXII (June, 1960), 15-20.

737. Lorenzen, Rudolf. "Manipulation verboten," *Berliner Leben*, No. 3 (1969).

738. Louvish, Misha. "Offener Brief an Günter Grass: Lassen Sie uns Zeit," *Die Zeit,* No. 49 (December 7, 1971), p. 10.

739. Loy, Leo. "Nicht besonders gelungen. SPD-Wahlkämpfer in Nürnberg," *Abendzeitung/8-Uhr-Blatt,*München (November 2, 1970).

740. Lucke, Fritz. "Ein Nachwort zu Günter Grass," *Nordwest-Zeitung*, Oldenburg (September 17, 1965).

741. Lucke, Hans. "Günter Grass' Novelle *Katz und Maus* im Unterricht," *Der Deutschunterricht,* XXI, 2 (1969), 86-95. (KuM)

742. Luft, Friedrich. "*Die Bösen Köche*—Uraufgeführt," *Die Welt*, No. 33 (February 21, 1961). (BK)

743. _____. "Ein Wallenstein der Revolution," *Die Welt*, No. 13 (January 17, 1966), p. 9. (Pl)

744. ________. "Fröhlich frecher Umgang mit dem Absurden," *Die Welt* (February 21, 1961). (BK)

745. ________. "Hier macht die Logik fröhlich Handstand," *Die Welt* (February 18, 1961), p. 17. (BK)

746. ________. "Die Plebejer proben den Aufstand," *Die Welt*, No. 13 (January 17, 1966), p. 9. (Pl)

747. Lummer, Heinrich. "Verzicht und Versöhnung," *Der Abend*, Berlin (December 7, 1970).

748. Luuk, Ernst and Jürgen Brinckmeier. "Kein Punkt Null in der Geschichte," *Berliner Stimme* (February 27, 1971).

749. Luyken, Sonja. "Onkel, Onkel," *Mannheimer Morgen* (March 6, 1958). (OO)

750. McGovern, Hugh. "Cat and Mouse," *America*, CIX, 11 (September 14, 1963), 264. (Rev, KuM)

751. ________. "The Tin Drum," *America*, CVIII, 10 (March 9, 1963), 344. (Bt)

752. Maier, Hansgeorg. "Powerteh der angestrengten Anstössigkeit," *Frankfurter Rundschau* (February 27, 1960), p. 3. (Bt)

753. Maier, Wolfgang. "Moderne Novelle," *Sprache im technischen Zeitalter*, I (October, 1961), 68-71. (KuM)

754. ________. "Die Unruhe um der Ruhe willen," *Berliner Morgenpost* (July 21, 1967). (Au)

755. Mann, Golo. "Hiergeblieben. Der Staat sind wir," *Frankfurter Allgemeine Zeitung* (May 18, 1968), p. 20.

756. Marbach, Renate. "Keine Scheu vor Meinungsstreit. Die NS-Spielart des Faschismus hat ja nicht mit Auschwitz angefangen," *Stuttgarter Nachrichten* (October 31, 1967).

757. Marcuse, Ludwig. "Es bleibt nur Schweigen," *Die Zeit,* No. 36 (September 1, 1961).

758. Masini, Ferruccio. "Günter Grass," *L'Unità,* Rome (September 17, 1966). (Hj)

759. Matsuda, Nobuo. "Die Komik in Günter Grass' Roman *Die Blechtrommel,*" *Doitsu Bungaku,* Tokyo, XXXV (October, 1965), pp. 1-11. (Bt)

760. Maurer, Robert. "The End of Innocence: Günter Grass' *The Tin Drum,*" *Bucknell Review,* XVI, 2 (May, 1968), 45-65. (Bt)

761. Mayer, Hans. "Dürrenmatts *Meteor* und Grass' *Die Plebejer,*" *Theater Heute,* VII, 3 (February, 1966), 23-26. (Pl)

762. _____. "Felix Krull und Oskar Matzerath," *Süddeutsche Zeitung,* München (October 14, 1967), p. 2. (Bt)

763. _____. "Das lyrische Tagebuch des Günter Grass," *Der Tagesspiegel,* Berlin (July 23, 1967), p. 5. (Au)

764. Mayer-Amery, Christian. "Gruppe 47 at Princeton," *Nation,* CCII, 20 (May 16, 1966), 588-589. (Gruppe 47)

765. Meckel, Eberhard. "Hundejahre," *Badische Zeitung,* Freiburg im Breisgau (December 30, 1963). (Hj)

766. Menzel, Claus. "Ein Billy Graham der Schreibmaschine," *Berliner Liberale Zeitung* (May 1, 1970).

767. Metzger-Hirt, Erika. "Günter Grass: 'Askese'," *Monatshefte,* LVII, 2 (Summer, 1965), 283-290.

768. Meyers, Hans. "Offener Brief," *Darmstädter Tagblatt* (September 30, 1965).

769. _____. "Unzüchtigkeit als kulturelles Gedankenspiel," *Darmstädter Tagblatt* (October 7, 1965).

770. Michaelis, Rolf. "Höllenfahrt mit Günter Grass," *Stuttgarter Zeitung* (September 7, 1963). (Hj)

771. Mieg, Peter. "Die Blechtrommel," *Badener Tagblatt* (February 12, 1960). (Bt)

772. Migner, Karl. "Der getrommelte Protest gegen unsere Welt," *Welt und Wort*, XV, 7 (July, 1960), 205-207. (Bt)

773. "Mit Recht und Freiheit richtig umgehen," *"Darmstädter Tagblatt* (October 19, 1965).

774. Mletschina, Irina. "Grass' Wrong Turn," *Atlas*, XII, 6 (December, 1966), 48-50.

775. _____. "Tertium non datur," *Sinn und Form*, XVIII, 4 (1966), 1258-1262. (Bt)

776. Morlock, Martin. "Die Schmutzigen Finger," *Der Spiegel*, XIX, 14 (March 29, 1965), 145.

777. Müller, André. "Realistisch im Detail, unrealistisch im Ganzen," *Die Tat*, Frankfurt am Main (December 7, 1963). (Hj)

778. Müller-Eckhard, P. "Die Blechtrommel," *Kölnische Rundschau* (December 13, 1959), p. 23. (Bt)

779. Murray, J. "Katz und Maus," *Critic*, XXII (October/November, 1963), 77. (Rev, KuM)

780. Muschg, Adolf. "Plädoyer für den falschen Drachen," *Die Zeit*, No. 27 (July 6, 1971). p. 11.

781. Nagel, Ivan. "Günter Grass' *Hundejahre*," *Die Zeit*, No. 5 (January 29, 1963), p. 27. (Hj)

782. Neuhaus, Volker. "Belle Tulla sans merci," *Arcadia*, V (1970), 278-295. (Hj)

783. Neveux, J.B. "Günter Grass le vistulien," *Études Germaniques*, XXI, 4 (1966), 527-550. (Hj)

784. Ni. "Grass: Hochwasser," *Generalanzeiger der Stadt Wuppertal* (February 8, 1960). (Hw)

785. Niehoff, Karena. "Die bösen Köche," *Süddeutsche Zeitung,* München (February 18, 1961). (BK)

786. Nöhbauer, Hans F. "Die grosse Danziger Hunde-Saga," *Abendzeitung,* München (August 10, 1963). (Hj)

787. ⸺⸺⸺⸺. "Joachim Mahlkes Vierklee," *Abendzeitung,* München (October 25, 1961). (KuM)

788. Nolte, Jost. "Baltisch, tückish, stubenwarm," *Die Welt* (April 13, 1967). (Au)

789. ⸺⸺⸺⸺. "Ich schreibe, denn das muss weg," *Die Welt* (October 19, 1961). (KuM)

790. ⸺⸺⸺⸺. "Menschen gequält von dieser Welt," *Die Welt* (December 2, 1960). (Gl)

791. ⸺⸺⸺⸺. "Oskar, der Trommler, kennt kein Tabu," *Die Welt* (October 17, 1959). (Bt)

792. ⸺⸺⸺⸺. "Die Plebejer proben den Aufstand," *Die Welt* (January 6, 1968). (Pl)

793. ⸺⸺⸺⸺. "Der Zeit in den schmutzigen Rachen gegriffen," *Die Welt* (September 7, 1963). (Hj)

794. "Nur mit der Zange anzufassen!" *Das Ritterkreuz,* Wiesbaden (April, 1962). (KuM)

795. Offenbach, Jürgen. "Ich bin doch kein Bürgerschreck. Der Schriftsteller glaubt: Nur die SPD garantiert Reformen," *Stuttgarter Nachrichten* (May 24, 1969).

796. Oliver, Edith. "Bravo pour le Clown!" *New Yorker,* XLII, 50 (February 4, 1967), 93ff. (BK)

797. ⸺⸺⸺⸺. "Off Broadway," *New Yorker,* XLII, 11 (May 7, 1966), 120-122.

798. O'Rourke, William. "Local Anaesthetic," *Nation,* CCX, 16 (April 27, 1970), 508. (Rev. öb)

799. Orzechowski, Lothar. "Kein Aufstand in der Ruine," *Hessische Allgemeine,* Kassel (July 11, 1966). (Pl)

800. Ottinger, Emil. "Denn was mit Katze und Maus begann, quält mich heute. . . ," *Eckart Jahrbuch*, CLXII (1964/1965), 231-237. (KuM)

801. _____. "Zur mehrdimensionalen Erklärung von Straftaten Jugendlicher am Beispiel der Novelle *Katz und Maus* von Günter Grass," *Monatsschrift für Kriminologie und Strafrechtsreform*, No. 5/6 (1962), pp. 175-183. (KuM)

802. Paoli, Rudolfo. "Günter Grass," *Il Tempo*, Rome (September 8, 1966). (Hj)

803. Parry, Idris. "Aspects of Günter Grass' Narrative Technique," *Forum for Modern Language Studies*, University of St. Andrews, Scotland, III (1967), 100-114.

804. _____. "The Special Quality of Hell," *Listener*, LXXV (February 3, 1966), 173-174. (Hj)

805. Pasolli, Robert. "The World of Günter Grass," *Nation*, CCII, 20 (May 16, 1966), 597-598.

806. Patera, Paul "Grass mot Brecht," *Horisont*, Vasa, XIII, 3 (1966), 80-83.

807. Petit, Henri. "Günter Grass," *Parisien libéré* (October 31, 1961).

808. Pfeiffer, John R. "*Katz und Maus*: Grass' Debt to Augustine," *Papers on Language and Literature*, VII, 3 (Summer, 1971), 279-292. (KuM)

809. Pfütze, Rudolf. "Grass und die deutsche Illusion," *Süddeutsche Zeitung*, München (July 1/2, 1967), p. 66.

810. Pickar, Gertrud Bauer. "The Aspect of Colour in Günter Grass' *Katz und Maus*," *German Life and Letters*, XXIII (1970), 304-309. (KuM)

811. _____. "Intentional ambiguity in Günter Grass' *Katz und Maus*," *Orbis litteratura*, XXVI (1971), 232-245. (KuM)

812. Piontek, Heinz. "Ein Gedicht und sein Autor," *Süddeutsche Zeitung*, München (December 7, 1967).

813. "Plans for Deutsche Oper Ballet Ensemble," *The German Tribune*, IX, 438 (September 3, 1970), 7. (Vo)

814. Plard, Henri. "Verteidigung der Blechtrommeln," *Text und Kritik*, I, 1 (1965), 1-8. (Bt)

815. Plavius, Heinz. "Geschwätz verhindert Taten," *Neue Deutsche Literatur*, XVII, 8 (1969), 173-178. (Rev, D)

816. "Plebeians Rehearse the Uprising," *Life*, LX, 17 (February 18, 1966). (Pl)

817. "The Poly-Papadoupoulos," *Time*, XCIX, 14 (April 3, 1972), 27-28.

818. Popkin, Henry. "Mr. Brecht over a big Barrel," *Life*, LX, 17 (February 18, 1966), 17. (Pl)

819. "Portrait of "Günter Grass," *Maclean's Magazine*, Toronto, LXXVIII (July 3, 1965), 47.

820. Postillion, Janice. "Third Reich, Legacies Set Literary Theme," *The Chronicle*, U.S. Army Command. Munich, Germany, XXI, 30 (March 10, 1967), 2. (Hj)

821. "Protest gegen Grass," *Darmstädter Tagblatt* (September 24, 1965).

822. Purwin, Hildegard. "In Leipzig und Frankfurt am Main," *Telegraf*, Berlin (May 31, 1967).

823. Rainer, Wolfgang. "Welt im Adamsapfel," *Der Tag*, Berlin (December 3, 1961). (KuM)

824. Rand, Max. "Günter Grass," *Unsi Suomi*, Helsinki (May 5, 1963). (Bt)

825. _____. "Günter Grass: *Katz und Maus*," *Unsi Suomi*, Helsinki (May 5, 1963). (KuM)

The Plebeians
Rehearse the Uprising

A German Tragedy

Günter Grass

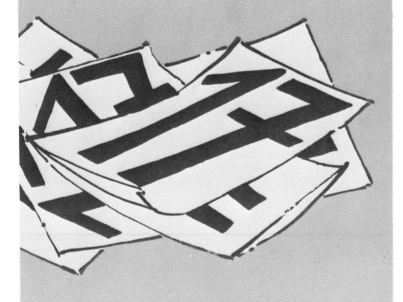

[Item no. 187]

826. Raymont, Henry. "Frankfurt: Buffoons and Tragedians," *American-German Review*, XXXV, 2 (New Year Issue, 1969), 13-17.

827. "Rebirth of German Letters Cited," *The Commercial Appeal*, Memphis, Tennessee (October 20, 1972), p. 2.

828. Redmond, James. "Günter Grass: A Kaschubian George Bernard Shaw," *Modern Drama*, No. 14 (1971/1972), pp. 104-113.

829. _____. "Günter Grass and (Der Fall Brecht)," *Modern Language Quarterly*, XXXII (1971), 387-400. (Pl)

830. Reich-Ranicki, Marcel. "Auf gut Glück getrommelt," *Die Zeit*, No. 1 (January 1, 1960), p. 20. (Bt)

831. _____. "Eine Diktatur, die wir befürworten," *Die Kultur*, München (November 15, 1958). (Gruppe 47).

832. _____. "Eine Müdeheldensosse," *Die Zeit*, No. 35 (September 2, 1969), p. 14. (öb)

833. _____. "Einhundertvierzig deutsche Dichter," *Die Zeit*, No. 12 (March 24, 1970), p. 9.

834. _____. "Die Geschichte des Ritterkreuzträgers," *Die Zeit*, No. 46 (November 10, 1961), p. 23. (KuM)

835. _____. "Hüben und Drüben. Goes, Grass, und Weiss," *Die Zeit*, No. 12 (March 19, 1965), p. 23.

836. _____. "Neue Gedichte von Günter Grass," *Die Zeit*, No. 20 (May 16, 1967). (Au)

837. _____. "Trauerspiel von einem deutschen Trauerspiel," *Die Zeit*, No. 4 (January 25, 1966), p. 9. (Pl)

838. Reif, Adelbert. "Der erste Schritt," *Spandauer Volksblatt*, Berlin (December 7, 1969).

839. —————————. "Rechts-Sprechung," *Welt der Arbeit*, Köln-Deutz (January 17, 1969).

840. Reiser, Hans. "Was ich wirklich gesagt habe. Der Schriftsteller nimmt Stellung zu den Vorwürfen der CSU, er habe im amerikanischen Fernsehen Bundeskanzler Kiesinger beschimpft," *Süddeutsche Zeitung,* Müncen (June 11, 1969).

841. Reisner, Stefan. "Der ungedruckte Grass," *Berliner Extra-Dienst* (June 5, 1971).

842. Reissmüller, Johann Georg. "Freischwebend," *Frankfurter Allgemeine Zeitung* (Sept. 18, 1965).

843. "Richters Richtfest," *Der Spiegel,* XVI, 44 (October 22, 1962), p. 73. (Gruppe 47).

844. Rieck, Horst. "Protest ohne Instinkte, AZ-Interview mit Günter Grass zur politischen Situation," *Abendzeitung/8-Uhr-Blatt,* München (6/20/'68)

845. Riehl, Hans. "Ein langer Marsch," *tz,* München (May 14, 1970).

846. Rischbieter, Henning. "Gespräch mit Günter Grass," *Theater Heute,* No. 4 (1969).

847. —————————. "Grass probt den Aufstand," *Theater Heute,* VII, 2 (February, 1966). (Pl)

847a. Robinson, Donald. *The 100 most important people in the world today.* (N.Y., Putnam, 1970), p.297.

848. Röhl, Klaus Rainer. "Grass in Weimar," *Konkret* (December, 1964).

849. —————————. "War Brecht Sozialdemokrat?" *Konkret* (February, 1966). (Pl)

850. Röllinghoff, Manfred. "Die NPD ist nur die Spitze eines Eisberges," *Main-Echo,* Aschaffenburg (May 29, 1969).

851. Roloff, Michael. "Books and Men: Günter Grass," *Atlantic,* CCXV, 6 (June 1965), 94-97. (Hj)

852. Roos, Peter. "Günter Grass-Interview," *Blechmusik*, Schülerzeitung des Mozartgymnasiums, Würzburg (December, 1969).

853. Rovit, Earl. "The Holy Ghost and the Dog," *American Scholar*, XXXIV, 3 (Fall, 1965), 676-684. (Hj)

854. Rp. "Hinter dem Guckloch," *Deutsche Volkszeitung*, Düsseldorf (April 8, 1960). (Bt)

855. Rühmkorf, Peter. "Erkenne die Marktlage!" *Sprache* 781-784.

856. Ruhleder, Karl H. "A Pattern of Messianic Thought in Günter Grass' *Cat and Mouse*," *The German Quarterly*, XXXIX, 4 (November, 1966), 599-612. (KuM)

857. Ryszka, Franciszek. "Günter Grass," *Wspólczesnośc̀*, Warsaw (1965), (Hj)

im technischen Zeitalter, No. 9.10 (1964), pp.

858. S., V. I. "Das Silvester WAZ-Gespräch," *Westdeutsche Allgemeine*, Gelsenkirchen (December 31, 1966).

859. Sabais, H.W. "Ich werde keine Antwort schuldig bleiben," *Darmstädter Tagblatt* (October 23, 1965).

860. Saller, Martin. "Ein Hetz-Pamphlet," *Hamburger Abendblatt* (September 26, 1967).

861. Schäble, Günter. "Die Ideologien haben versagt. Interview der *Stuttgarter Zeitung* mit Günter Grass," *Stuttgarter Zeitung* (February 18, 1969).

862. Scharnagl, Wilfried. "Der letzte Kredit steht auf dem Spiel," *Bayern-Kurier*, München (October 7, 1967).

863. Scheller, Wolf. "Nicht so primitiv," *Spandauer Volksblatt*, Berlin (June 22, 1969).

864. Scherman, David E. "Green Years for Günter Grass," *Life*, LVIII, 22 (June 4, 1965), 51-56. (Hj)

865. Schimming. W. "Die Plebejer proben den Aufstand," *Allgemeine Zeitung*, Mainz (January 15, 1966). (Pl)

866. "Der Schlag auf die Blechtrommel," *Weser-Kurier*, Bremen (December 30, 1959).

867. Schlamm, William S. "Der SDS und die SA," *Salzburger Nachrichten* (February 17, 1968).

868. Schlocker, Georges. "Une pièce de Günter Grass," *Lettres Nouvelles* (March/April, 1966), pp. 136-139.

869. Schmidt, Dietmar. "Tauziehen um Kipphardt," *Die Welt* (May 15, 1971).

870. Schmidt, Klaus. "CDU-Spitze gegen die Aktion der Jungen Union," *Darmstädter Echo* (September 25, 1965).

871. Schneider, Peter. "Individuelle Sachlichkeit," *Kürbiskern*, München (January, 1968). (Au)

872. "Der schöne Schein," *Deutsche Zeitung,* Köln (February 6/7, 1960).

873. Scholz, Hans. "Schildernder, bildernder Auerdichter," *Der Tagesspiegel*, Berlin (September 1, 1963). (Hj)

874. Schonauer, Franz. "Kindertrommel und die schwarze Köchin," *Stuttgarter Nachrichten* (October 17, 1959). (Bt)

875. Schüler, Alfred. "Coriolan und Stalinallee," *Die Weltwoche*, Zürich (January 21, 1966). (Pl)

876. Schüler, Gerhard. "Katz und Maus," *Süd-Kurier*, Konstanz (December 30, 1961). (KuM)

877. _____. "Onkel, Onkel," *Göttinger Tageblatt* (June 1, 1961). (OO)

878. Schulz, Uwe. "Auskunft über die Ohnmacht," *Frankfurter Rundschau* (August 12, 1967). (Au)

879. Schumann. Willy. "Wiederkehr der Schelme," *Publication of the Modern Language Association*, LXXXI, 7 (December, 1966), 467-474. (Pl)

880. Schuster, Hans. "Die deutsche Unruhe," *Süddeutsche Zeitung*, München (June 16, 1967).

881. Schwab-Felisch, Hans. "Dichter auf dem 'elektrischen Stuhl'," *Frankfurter Allgemeine Zeitung*, Literaturblatt (November 1, 1956). (Gruppe 47)

882. _____. "Eine Trauerspiel," *Frankfurter Allgemeine Zeitung* (December 29, 1959).

883. _____. "Günter Grass und der 17. Juni," *Merkur*, XX, 3 (March, 1966), 291-294. (Pl)

884. _____. "örtlich betäubt," *Merkur*, XXIII (1969), 776-779. (Rev, öb)

885. _____. "Zweimal Zeitgeschichte in Düsseldorf," *Süddeutsche Zeitung,* München (January 25, 1967), p. 15. (Pl)

886. Schwedhelm, Karl. "Aus vollem Hals erzählt," *St. Galler Tagblatt* (September 8, 1963). (Hj)

887. _____. "Danziger schweres Goldwasser," *St. Galler Tagblatt* (November 19, 1961). (KuM)

888. Segebrecht, Dietrich. "Dialektik oder das Vorbild der Kochkunst," *Frankfurter Allgemeine Zeitung*, Literaturblatt (March 14, 1967). (Au)

889. _____. "Günter Grass: *Katz und Maus*," *Bücherei und Bildung,* II (February, 1962), 73-75 (KuM)

890. _____. "Kein neues Bissgefühl," *Frankfurter Allgemeine Zeitung*, Literaturblatt (August 16, 1969). (öb)

891. Segebrecht, Wulf. "Für prüde Gemüter ungeeignet," *Vorwärts*, Bonn (February 17, 1961), p. 6. (Gl)

892. Seidler, Ingo. "Rainer Maria Rilke und Günter Grass: Zwei Gedichte oder eines?" *International Arthur Schnitzler Research Association Journal*, II, 4 (1963), 4-10.

893. Serke, Jürgen. "Pornographie und blasphemie sind keine literarischen begriffe. Ein gespräch mit Günter Grass—andrej wadja verfilmt die novelle *Katz und Maus*," *Kultur* (October 14, 1963).

894. Seyppel, Joachim. "Offener Brief an Günter Grass," *Die Wahrheit*, Berlin (January 29, 1971).

895. Sharfman, William L. "The Organization of Experience in *The Tin Drum*," *Minnesota Review*, VI, 1 (1966), 59-65. (Bt)

896. Short, Susan. "Günter Grass, Lyriker," *Guardian* (July 15, 1967), p. 4.

897. Siering, Joseph. "Hundejahre," *Neue Deutsche Hefte*, X, 96 (1963), 131-134. (Rev, Hj)

898. Singer, Herbert. "Die Nachteile der Windeier," *Neue Deutsche Hefte*, VIII, 79 (1962), 1025-1026. (Gl)

899. Smith, M. A. "*The Tin Drum* by Günter Grass," *Kolokon*, II (Spring, 1967), 48-52. (Rev, Bt)

900. Smith, William James. "The Stage," *Commonweal*, LXXXV, 19 (February 2, 1967), 567ff. (BK)

901. Sobotta, Joachim. "Gerangel mit Günter Grass," *Rheinische Post*, Düsseldorf (March 21, 1969).

902. _____. "Zwei Danziger," *Rheinische Post*, Düsseldorf (March 20, 1968).

903. Sokolov, R.A. "Voice of Grass," *Newsweek*, LXXIII, 21 (May 26, 1969), 120ff.

904. Sosnoski, M.K. "Oskar's Hungry Witch," *Modern Fiction Studies*, XVII, 1 (Spring, 1971), 61-80. (Bt)

905. "Sowas durchmachen," *Der Spiegel*, XXIII, 33 (August 11, 1969), 86ff.

906. "A Sow-er Note for Diners," *The Stars and Stripes*, European Edition (April 5, 1970), p. 4.

907. Spaethling, Robert H. "Günter Grass: *Cat and Mouse*," *Monatshefte*, LXII, 2 (Summer, 1970), 141-153. (KuM)

908. Spender, Stephen. "Cat and Mouse," *New York Times* (August 11, 1963). (KuM)

909. _____. "Günter Grass," *The Sunday Telegraph*, London (September 30, 1962). (Bt)

910. "Springers Ablenkungsmanöver," *Die Andere Zeitung*, Hamburg (October 5, 1967).

911. Spycher, Peter. "*Die bösen Köche* von Günter Grass—Ein 'absurdes' Drama?" *Germanisch-romanische Monatsschrift*, XVI (1966), 161-189. (BK)

912. Steffen, Jochen. "Gewalt ist Schiessgewehr," Der *Spiegel*, XXV, 27 (June 28, 1971).

913. Steig, Michael. "The Grotesque and the aesthetic response in Shakespeare, Dickens, and Günter Grass," *Contemporary Literature Studies*, VI (1969), 167-181.

914. Steiner, George. "The Nerve of Günter Grass," *Commentary*, XXXVII, 5 (May, 1964), 77-80.

915. Stephan, Charlotte. "Junge Autoren unter sich," *Der Tagesspiegel*, Berlin (May 17, 1955). (Gruppe 47)

916. "Der Stich ins Wespennest," *Die Zeit*, No. 36 (September 1, 1961).

917. Stiller, Klaus. "Mann kann nicht bei der Nein-Position stehenbleiben. Interview mit dem Schrifsteller Günter Grass," *Frankfurter Rundschau* (March 10, 1969).

918. Stomps, Victor Otto. "Menschenjahre-Hundejahre," *Text und Kritik*, I, 1 (1965), 9-12. (Hj)

919. Stone, M. "Günter Grass," *Saturday Review*, XLVII (May 29, 1965), 26.

920. "Strafanzeige gegen Günter Grass," *BILD*, Berlin (September 28, 1969).

921. Suttner, Hans. "Blechtrommler auf Tournee," *Echo der Zeit*, Recklinghausen, No. 29 (July 18, 1965), pp. 20-22.

922. _____. "Der leider misslungene Versuch Günter Grass politisch zu verstehen," *Echo der Zeit*, Recklinghausen, No. 30 (July 25, 1965), pp. 27-30.

923. Sutton, Ellen. "Grass and Bobrowski," *London Times Literary Supplement* (February 17, 1966), p. 123.

924. Tank, Kurt Lothar. "Der Blechtrommler schrieb Memoiren," *Welt am Sonntag,* Hamburg (October 4, 1959). (Bt)

925. _____. "Die Diktatur der Vogelscheuchen," *Sonntagsblatt,* Hamburg (September 1, 1963). (Hj)

926. _____. "Ein deutsches Trauerspiel—durchgerechnet von Günter Grass," *Sonntagsblatt, Hamburg* (January 23, 1966). (Pl)

927. Tasch, Dieter. "Cloppenburg fand Grass verändert," *Hannoversche Allgemeine* (August 29, 1969).

928. Thiess, Frank. "Der Krach mit den 'Pinschern'," *Die Allgemeine Sonntagszeitung*, Würzburg (August 22, 1965).

929. Todd, Olivier. "Le chat et la souris," *France Observateur*, Paris (October 17, 1962). (KuM)

930. Toeppen, Hans. "Hundejahre für die Berliner Schule? Ein Interview mit Günter Grass zum Rücktritt von Senator Evers," *Der Tagesspiegel*, Berlin (March 6, 1970).

931. Traynor, J. "Katz und Maus," *Extension*, LVIII (January, 1964), 43. (Rev, KuM)

932. Triesch, Manfred. "Günter Grass: *Die Plebejer proben den Aufstand*," *Books Abroad*, XL, 3 (Summer, 1966), 285-287. (Pl)

933. "Der Trommelbube," *Der Spiegel*, XIII, 47 (November 16, 1959), 41. (Bt)

934. Ude, Karl. "Günter Grass und das Christentum," *Welt und Wort*, XXIV, 6 (June, 1969), 180.

935. Uhlig, Helmut, "Die Trommel ist sein Tick," *Der Tag*, Berlin (September 13, 1959). (Bt)

936. "Unflätiger Grass," *Das Deutsche Wort*, Köln (September 1, 1963). (Hj)

937. Ungureit, Heinz. "Da wären die Hundejahre," *Frankfurter Rundschau* (August 31, 1963). (Hj)

938. Uplike, J. "View from the Dental Chair," *New Yorker*, XLVI, 10 (April 25, 1970). (öb)

939. Urbach, Ilse. "Der Aufstand tritt auf der Stelle," *Der Kurier*, Berlin (January 17, 1966). (Pl)

940. _____. "Scharfes Süppchen von Günter Grass," *Der Kurier*, Berlin (February 17, 1961). (BK)

941. Van Abbé, Derek. "Metamorphoses of 'Unbewältigte Vergangenheit' in *Die Blechtrommel*," *German Life and Letters*, XXIII (January, 1970), 152-160. (Bt)

942. Verbeeck, Ludo. "Günter Grass tussen roman en pamflet," *Dietsche Warande & Belfort*, CXV (1970), 677-688.

943. Vetter, Hans. "Ein Spruchkammer-Kabarett über die Hitlerschen Hundstage," *Kölner Stadt-Anzeiger* (August 17, 1963). (Hj)

944. Vielhaber, Gerd. "Günter Grass und die Folgen," *Frankfurter Allgemeine Zeitung*, Literaturblatt (January 19, 1967). (Pl)

945. Vogel, Dieter. "Grass empfiehlt die SPD als Hotelfrühstücksreformer," *Frankfurter Allgemeine Zeitung* (July 10, 1965).

946. von B., C. "Das Establishment braucht Provokation. AZ-Gespräch mit Günter Grass," *Abendzeitung/8-Uhr-Blatt,* München (February 4, 1969).

947. _____. "Ich kenne das Rezept auch nicht. Gespräch mit Günter Grass," *Wiesbadener Kurier* (February 4, 1969).

948. von Berg, Robert. "Die Kunst, eine Suppe zu versalzen," *Die Tat*, Zürich (February 4, 1967). (BK)

949. von Freiburg, E. R. "Half and Half Equals Two," *Nation*, CCIV, 16 (April 17, 1967), 503-506.

950. von Hassel, Kai Uwe. "Günter Grass begreift es nicht," *Die Welt* (October 2, 1967).

951. von Oppen, B.R. "Two German Writers of the Sixties," *Massachusetts Review*, V, 4 (Summer, 1964), 769-778. (Bt)

952. von Puttkamer, Jesco. "Ein Schriftsteller engagiert sich," *Vorwärts*, Bonn (July 28, 1965).

953. von und zu Guttenberg, Freiherr Karl Theodor. "Vom Trommler zum Tambourmajor," *Abendzeitung*, München (December 22, 1966).

954. von Vegesack, Thomas. "Danzig I Världslitteraturen," *Stockholms Tidningen* (November 20, 1961). (Bt)

955. Vormweg, Heinrich. "Apokalypse mit Vogelscheuchen," *Deutsche Zeitung,* Köln (August 31, 1963). (Hj)

956. _____. "Der Berühmte," *Magnum Jahresheft,* Köln (1964).

957. _____. "Gedichtsschreiber Grass," *Akzente,* XVII, 405-416.

958. _____. "Keine Antwort für Günter Grass," *CIVIS,* Bonn (January 1, 1967).

959. "Der Wähler soll mitbestimmen. Interview mit dem Schriftsteller Günter Grass," *Hamburger Morgenpost* (August 30, 1969).

960. Wagenbach, Klaus. "Günter Grass: *Katz und Maus,*" *Evangelischer Literaturbeobachter,* München, No. 44 (December, 1961), pp. 882-883. (KuM)

961. _____. "Jens Tadelt zu Unrecht," *Die Zeit,* No. 38 (November 17, 1963), p. 8. (Hj)

962. Walden, Matthias. "Günter Grass und die 'linksgewickelten Narren'," *Welt am Sonntag,* Hamburg (June 6, 1971).

963. _____. "Wie grauslich ist die Politik?" *Die Welt*(September 13, 1969).

964. Wallman, Jürgen P. "Günter Grass: *Hundejahre,*" *Die Tat,* Zürich (September 6, 1963). (Hj)

965. Wallraf, Karlheinz. "Umstrittene Bücher. Günter Grass: *Katz und Maus,*" *Bücherei und Bildung,* No. 4 (April, 1962), pp. 186ff. (KuM)

966. Walser, Martin. "Deutsche Schussrichtung," *Die Zeit,* No. 23 (May 28, 1971).

967. _____. "Soll man diese Nieren essen?" *Die Zeit,* No. 10 (March 2, 1962).

968. Wapnewski, Peter, "Einst hiessen sie Gruppe 47," *Die Zeit,* No. 18 (May 9, 1972), p. 10. (Gruppe 47)

969. Weber, Werner. "Örtlich betäubt," *Der Monat*, XXI, 253 (1969), 94-98. (Rev, öb)

970. Wegener, Adolph. "Lyrik und Graphik von Günter Grass," *Philobiblon*, X, 2 (1966), 110-118.

971. Weitz, Werner. "Nie gegen das christliche Ethos. Fragen an den Autor Günter Grass," *Würzburger Katholisches Sonntagsblatt* (July 27, 1969).

972. Wendt, Ernst. "Sein grosses Ja bildet Sätze mit kleinem Nein," *Theater Heute*, VIII, 4 (April 4, 1967), 6-11.

973. Wessel, Kurt. "Der faschistische Qualm," *Münchner Merkur* (September 30, 1967).

974. _____. "Örtlich betäubt," *Europa-Report*, No. 9 (1969), pp. 52-53. (Rev, öb)

975. "West German novelist wins Nobel Prize," *The Oxford Eagle*, Oxford, Mississippi (October 19, 1972), p. 10A.

976. "West German People rated by Novelist," *Baton Rouge Morning Advocate* (February 3, 1969), p. 3-A.

977. West, Paul. "The Grotesque Purgation," *Nation*, CCI, 4 (August 16, 1965), 81-84. (Hj)

978. Weyrauch, Wolfgang. "Ausgefragt: Was heisst das?" *Tribüne*, Frankfurt am Main (September, 1967). (Au)

979. "Wicked Cooks," *Commonweal*, LXXXV, 19 (February 17, 1967), 567. (Rev, BK)

980. Widmer, Walter. "Baal spielt Katz und Maus," *National-Zeitung*, Basel (December 19, 1961). (KuM)

981. _____. "Geniale Verruchtheit," *Basler Nachrichten* (December 18, 1959). (Bt)

982. Wiegenstein, Roland H. "Noch ein Vorschlag, Günter Grass zu verstehen," *Frankfurter Hefte*, No. 18 (1963), pp. 870-873. (Hj)

983. Wien, Werner. "Trauermarsch auf der Blechtrommel," *Christ und Welt* (December 17, 1959). (Bt)

984. _____. "Der vorbestellte Erfolg," *Darmstädter Echo* (October 4, 1963). (Hj)

985. Wieser, Theodor: *"Die Blechtrommel: Fabulierer und Moralist,"* *Merkur*, XIII, 12 (December 1959), 1188-1191. (Bt)

986. Wijmark, Carl-Henning. "Günter Grass," *Vandringar Med Böker*, Lund, XVII, 8 (1968), 1-4.

987. Willson, A. Leslie. "The Grotesque Everyman in *Die Blechtrommel*," *Monatshefte*, LVIII, 2 (Summer, 1966), 131-138. (Bt)

988. _____. "Perspective: The Dance of Art," *Dimension*, III, Special Issue (1970), 7-21.

989. Wimmer, Ernst. "Warum das Burgtheater ausgerechnet Grass spielt," *Die Wahrheit*, Graz (February 19, 1966). (Pl)

990. Wintzen, René. "Günter Grass le Non-Conformist," *Documents*, Paris (March/April, 1964).

991. Wirth, Andrzej. "Günter Grass and the Dilemma of Documentary Drama," *Dimension*, III, Special Issue (1970), 22-35. (Pl)

992. Wolfheim, Hans. "Trommelexcesse der Literatur," *Hamburger Echo* (January 16,1960). (Bt)

993. Wolken, Karl Alfred. "Bis zum Anbruch der Müdigkeit," *Christ und Welt* (October 11, 1963). (Hj)

994. _____. "Neues aus der Kaschubei," *Christ und Welt* (October 20, 1961). (KuM)

995. Woods, Jean M. "Günter Grass: A Selected Bibliography," *West Coast Review*, V, 3 (1970), 52-56; VI, 1 (1971), 31-40

996. Woodtli, Susanna. "Die Blechtrommel," *Reformatio*, XI (1962), 365-369. (Bt)

997. Zampa, Georgio. "Günter Grass," *La Stampa*, Rome (January 22, 1964). (KuM)

998. Zielinski, Hans. "Die unbequemen Fragen des Günter Grass," *Die Welt*, No. 123 (May 30, 1961). (KuM)

999. Ziesel, Kurt. "Botschafter Grass," *Deutsche Tagespost*, Würzburg.

1000. "Ziesels Dank an CSU-Abgeordnete," dpa Announcement (May 9, 1969).

1001. Zimmer, Dieter E. "Deutsche Querelen," *Die Zeit*, No. 35 (September 5, 1972), pp. 9-10.

1002. —————. "Ein Verlag der Autoren" *Die Zeit*, No. 9 (March 4, 1969), p. 9.

1003. —————. "Interview with Günter Grass," *Encounter*, XXX, 1 (January, 1968), 71-74.

1004. —————. "Kriechspur des Günter Grass," *Die Zeit*, No. 40 (October 10, 1972), pp. 25-26. (TS)

1005. —————. "Politik interessiert zur Zeit mehr," *Die Zeit*, No. 43 (October 27, 1967), p. 17.

1005a. Zimmer, S. K. "Gdanski Tryptyk," *Wiadomsci*, London (July, 1971), pp. 4-11.

1006. Zimmermann, Werner. "Von Ernst Wiechert zu Günter Grass," *Wirkendes Wort*, XV (1965), 316-326.

1007. Zipes, Jack. "An Interview with Günter Grass," *University Review*, New York (May, 1969).

1008. Zundel, Rolf. "Mit der Macht auf du und du," *Die Zeit*, No. 17 (April 29, 1969), p. 4.

1009. _____. "Die SPD ist verstört," *Die Zeit*, No. 20 (May 20, 1969), p. 4

1010. Zwerenz, Gerhard. "Brecht, Grass und der 17. Juni," *Theater Heute,* VII, 3 (March, 1966), 24. (Pl)

1011. _____. "Hetze statt Information," *Metall*, Frankfurt am Main (October 16, 1967).

Unpublished Material

1012. Becker, Jürgen. "Gleisdreieck," Radio Speech, *Westdeutscher Rundfunk*, Köln (February 15, 1961). (Gl)

1013. Berets, Ralph Adolph. *The irrational narrator in Virginia Woolf's "The Waves," William Faulkner "The Sound and the Fury," and Günter Grass "The Tin Drum".* Dissertation Abstract, 31:751A, University of Michigan, 1969. (Bt)

1014. Damian, Hermann Siegfried. *"Die Blechtrommel" von Günter Grass. Versuch einer analyse.*M.A. Dissertation, University of Tasmania, 1967. (Bt)

1015. Everett, George Alexander, Jr. "Günter Grass and the Instruction of Youth," Paper given at the Biannual Meeting of the Mississippi Modern Language Association, Wesson, Mississippi, November 6, 1971.

1016. _____. Interview with Günter Grass, April 29, 1967, at his home, Niedstrasse 13, Berlin, West Germany.

1017. _____. *Preceptive Intent in the Works of Günter Grass: An Investigation and Assessment with Extensive Bibliography.* Dissertation Abstract, 32: 2683A, Louisiana State University, 1971.

1018. _____. *Swift's "Gulliver's Travels" and Grass' "Die Blechtrommel".* M.A. Thesis, Louisiana State University, 1966. (Bt)

1019. Ferguson, Lore Schefter. *"Die Blechtrommel" von Günter Grass: Versuch einer Interpretation.* Dissertation Abstract, 28:1074A, Ohio State University, 1967. (Bt)

1019a. Fuz, George C. "Judicial murder of the defenders of the Polish Post in the Free City of Danzig in 1939," Lecture delivered in New York City (April, 1971).

1020. "Die Hundejahre des Günter Grass, " Radio Speech, *Berliner Welle* (November 27, 1963). (Hj)

1021. "Interview with Günter Grass," *NET Television Network*, Channel 8 TV, New Orleans, Louisiana (October, 1967).

1022. "Interview with Günter Grass," The Today Show, NBC Television Network (March 17, 1970).

1023. Krolow, Karl. "Gleisdreieck," Radio Speech, *Südwestfunk*, Baden-Baden (March 29, 1961). (Gl)

1024. Latzel, Siegbert. "Grass als Lyriker," Tape Recording, Goethe Institute, München, 1972.

1025. Mason, Ann Lois. *Günter Grass' Conception of the Artist.* Dissertation Abstract, 32:443A, Cornell University, 1971.

1026. Melchinger, Siegfried. "Interpretation des Stückes *Die Plebejer proben den Aufstand* von Günter Grass," Tape Recording, Goethe Institute, München, 1972. (Pl)

1027. Moore, David Pittman. *Günter Grass and Alejandro Nuñez Alonso: A Comparative Study of their Novels.* Dissertation Abstract, 32:977A, University of Arkansas, 1971.

1028. Motekat, Helmut. "Zur Technik der Interpretation des modernen Romans:Ein Versuch an Günter

Grass' *Die Blechtrommel*," Tape Recording, Goethe Institute, München, 1971 (Bt)

1029. Nöhbauer, Hans F. "Wie ein Roman entsteht," Radio Speech, *Bayrischer Rundfunk*, München (February 22, 1968).

1030. Read, Ralph R. " 'Kann man den Shakespeare ändern?' In Defense of Grass' *Die Plebejer proben den Aufstand*," Paper given at the 27th Annual Meeting of the South Central Modern Language Association, Memphis, Tennessee, October 29-31, 1970. (Pl)

1031. Ritter, Jesse Paul, Jr. *Fearful Comedy: The Fiction of Joseph Heller, Günter Grass and the Social Surrealist Genre*. Dissertation Abstract, 28: 1447A, University of Arkansas, 1967.

1032. Stomps, Victor Otto. "Hundejahre," Radio Speech, *RIAS*, Berlin (January 25, 1964). (Hj)

1033. Uhlig, Helmut. "Realitäten, Humor und feine Ironie," Radio Speech, *Sender Freies Berlin* (August 2, 1956). (VW)

1034. Völker, Klaus. " 'Kinderlied' von Günter Grass," Radio Speech, *Sender Freies Berlin* (October 15, 1961). (Gl)

1035. Wagenbach, Klaus. "Marginalie," Radio Speech, *Bayrischer Rundfunk*, München (March 29, 1963).

1036. Wiegenstein, Roland H. "Hundejahre," Radio Speech. *Westdeutscher Rundfunk*, Köln (October 28, 1963). (Hj)

SUBJECT INDEX TO
THE CRITICAL LITERATURE

SUBJECT INDEX TO CRITICAL LITERATURE

LITERARY GENRES

Poetry

247, 248, 267, 288, 295, 310, 313, 334, 382, 410, 428, 481, 484, 485, 546, 552, 553, 582, 627, 633, 646, 688, 695, 696, 699, 703, 717, 723, 728, 754, 763, 767, 788, 790, 812, 836, 871, 878, 888, 891, 892, 896, 898, 957, 970, 978.

Prose

245, 246, 255, 258, 260, 261, 262, 270, 282, 283, 285, 291, 292, 293, 302, 307, 314, 321, 323, 329, 331, 335, 340, 343, 344, 352, 354, 355, 358, 359, 369, 375, 376, 377, 379, 380, 385, 386, 388, 389, 390, 391, 392, 393, 394, 395, 399, 401, 402, 404, 405, 411, 412, 413, 414, 416, 417, 424, 425, 426, 430, 437, 438, 439, 442, 443, 444, 445, 449, 452, 457, 458, 459, 462, 464, 465, 467, 471, 472, 474, 486, 487, 489, 491, 493, 498, 508, 518, 523, 526, 531, 532, 541, 543, 544, 547, 549, 551, 554, 556, 557, 559, 562, 563, 564, 568, 574, 578, 579, 589, 591, 594, 596, 599, 603, 605, 606, 607, 610, 625, 629, 632, 634, 635, 638, 641, 650, 652, 653, 656, 660, 661, 663, 664, 666, 667, 670, 676, 677, 679, 685, 689, 692, 697, 698, 702, 704, 706, 711, 712, 714, 715, 719, 724, 731, 732, 733, 735, 741, 744, 745, 750, 751, 752, 753, 758, 759, 760, 762, 765, 770, 771, 772, 775, 777, 778, 779, 781, 782, 783, 786, 787, 789, 791, 793, 794, 798, 800, 801, 802, 804, 808, 810, 814, 820, 823, 824, 825, 830, 832, 834, 851, 853, 854, 856, 857, 864, 873, 874, 876, 884, 886, 887, 889, 890, 893, 895, 897, 899, 904, 907, 908, 909, 918, 924, 925, 929, 931, 933, 935, 936, 937, 938, 941, 943, 951, 954, 955, 960, 961, 964, 965, 969, 974, 977, 980, 981, 982, 983, 984, 985, 987, 992, 993, 994, 996, 997, 998, 1004.

Drama

306, 315, 317, 342, 351, 353, 372, 383, 387, 403, 408, 418, 429, 433, 446, 448, 461, 463, 466, 468, 482, 500, 503, 506, 510, 515,

519, 539, 540, 545, 550, 555, 561, 583, 584, 585, 586, 587, 609,
612, 616, 626, 636, 642, 644, 647, 649, 659, 662, 672, 673, 674,
680, 690, 715, 726, 742, 743, 746, 749, 761, 784, 785, 792, 796,
797, 799, 805, 806, 813, 815, 816, 818, 828, 829, 837, 846, 847,
865, 875, 877, 879, 883, 885, 900, 911, 926, 932, 939, 940, 944,
948, 979, 989, 991, 1010.

BIOGRAPHY

266, 269, 332, 477, 538 598, 683, 687, 700, 716, 817, 819, 906.

LITERARY TECHNIQUE

249, 252, 256, 265, 271, 274, 275, 277, 280, 281, 284, 286, 294,
299, 300, 303, 308, 309, 336, 341, 356, 363, 370, 371, 398, 400,
415, 422, 423, 475, 476, 502, 592, 615, 622, 623, 630, 631, 640,
673, 683, 716, 717, 803, 810, 811, 895, 913, 914, 941, 971, 972,
988, 1001.

GRASS' WORLD OUTLOOK
POLITICAL AND SOCIAL THOUGHT

242, 253, 254, 276, 346, 348, 350, 360, 362, 365, 368, 373, 374,
378, 381, 384, 396, 397, 406, 407, 409, 421, 427, 431, 432, 434,
435, 436, 441, 450, 451, 454, 455, 456, 460, 473, 480, 483, 490,
492, 495, 496, 497, 499, 504, 505, 507, 509, 514, 516, 517, 520,
521, 522, 525, 527, 528, 529, 530, 535, 537, 558, 560, 565, 566,
569, 570, 571, 573, 575, 576, 577, 580, 581, 597, 600, 608, 611,
614, 617, 618, 619, 628, 639, 645, 651, 657, 658, 664, 665, 669,
671, 675, 678, 681, 683, 684, 686, 691, 693, 701, 705, 707, 709,
713, 718, 720, 722, 725, 727, 729, 738, 739, 740, 747, 748, 755,
756, 757, 766, 768, 769, 773, 780, 795, 808, 809, 821, 822, 826,

827, 838, 839, 840, 841, 842, 844, 848, 849, 850, 858, 859, 860,
861, 862, 863, 866, 867, 869, 870, 872, 880, 882, 894, 901, 902,
910, 912, 916, 917, 920, 921, 922, 927, 928, 930, 934, 945, 946,
947, 950, 952, 953, 958, 959, 962, 963, 966, 967, 971, 973, 976,
999, 1000, 1005, 1008, 1009, 1011.

GENERAL

240, 241, 243, 244, 250, 251, 257, 259, 263, 264, 268, 272, 273,
278, 279, 287, 289, 290, 296, 297, 298, 301, 304, 305, 311, 312,
316, 318, 319, 320, 322, 324, 325, 326, 327, 328, 330, 333, 337,
338, 339, 345, 347, 349, 357, 361, 364, 366, 367, 419, 420, 440,
447, 453, 469, 470, 478, 479, 488, 494, 501, 511, 512, 513, 524,
533, 534, 536, 542, 548, 567, 572, 588, 590, 593, 595, 601, 602,
604, 613, 620, 621, 624, 637, 643, 648, 654, 655, 668, 682, 694,
708, 710, 713, 721, 730, 734, 736, 737, 764, 774, 776, 807, 831,
833, 835, 843, 845, 852, 855, 868, 881, 903, 905, 915, 919, 923,
942, 949, 956, 968, 975, 986, 990, 995, 1002, 1003, 1006, 1007.